SAFARI CHIC

Wild Exteriors and
Polished Interiors of Africa

TEXT AND PHOTOGRAPHS
BY BIBI JORDAN

For my mother,
Agnes Mary Jordan:
parce que "tu as du chic!"

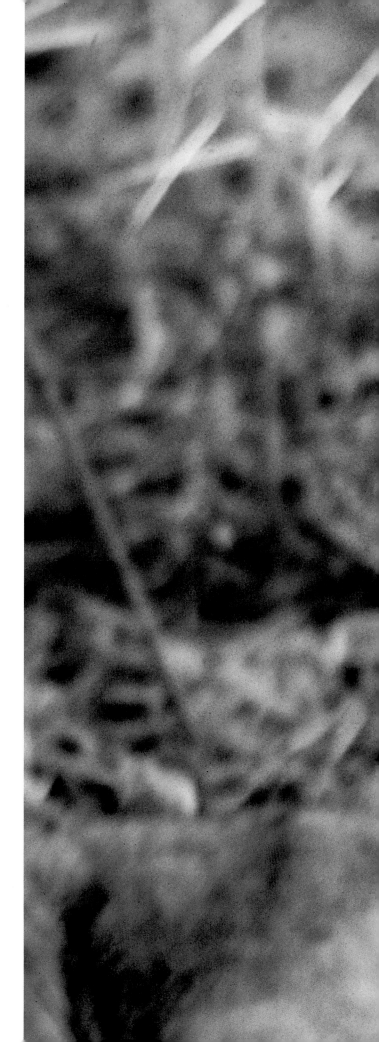

First Edition
05 04 03 02 01 00   5 4 3 2 1

Published by
Gibbs Smith, Publisher
P.O. Box 667
Layton, Utah 84041

Orders: (1-800) 748-5439
Website: www.gibbs-smith.com

Front cover photograph by Horst Klemm
Printed in China

Library of Congress Cataloging-in-Publication Data
Jordan, Bibi
    Safari chic : wild exteriors and polished interiors of Africa / by
Bibi Jordan.
        p.   cm.
    Includes bibliographical references.
    ISBN 0-87905-973-7 (hc)
    1. Safari lodges—Africa, Sub-Saharan. 2. Interior decoration—
Africa, Sub-Saharan. 3. Safaris—Africa, Sub-Saharan. I. Title.
NK2195.S24J67 2000
747—dc21   98-036580

SAFARI CHIC

Wild Exteriors and
Polished Interiors of Africa

TEXT AND PHOTOGRAPHS
BY BIBI JORDAN

"Always something new...
out of Africa."

—Pliny

acknowledgments

I went to Africa in search of a story, a style, and an adventure. I found it all. More importantly, on the road and around the campfires, I found friends. The magnetic personality, sense of adventure, and commitment to ideals of the "safari set" became infused in the project and, on my return, I found the book continued to draw a circle of friends and colleagues around me without whose support this book would not have materialized.

For their hospitality and indulgence, I want to thank all who welcomed me to their camps and showed me their Africa. Among the many people (in no particular order and certainly not all) who offered their friendship were Anne and Horst Klemm, Calvin Cottar, Maureen Cottar, Peter and Lou Behr, Alexandra France, Catherine Raphaely, Ralph Bousefield, Cobra, Supra, Betty Leslie-Melville, Gianna and Bruno Brighetti, Tony, Susan, and Gordon Church, Oria and Iain Douglas-Hamilton, Mike Rattray, Nick Wood, Mike Patterson, Lesley Simpson, Peter Frank, Pierre Mourgue d'Algue, Stephanie Kuna, Carla Pretorios, Randall Moore, Sandor Carter, Wayne McLintock, Nancy Galloway, Duncan and Louise Rodgers, Paul and Christophe Verleysen, David Brightman, Ben Parker, Sandy and Chip Cunningham, and Richard and Tara Bonham.

This book would not have been possible without the expert travel advice of Bush Homes/African Safaris. Travel to and within Africa was hassle-free thanks to Travel Spirit, who booked my flights, and Abercrombie and Kent, who provided flawless travel coordination within Africa. Classic Safari Camps and Conservation Corporation of Africa were also among those who graciously hosted me at many of the finest camps in Africa.

When my own confidence failed, my friends and family didn't: Cherie Briggs, Marie Sebastian, Marie Bardin, Nicolette Clark, and Bruce Schultz coaxed me on; Jennifer Hanna, Penny Randall, my sisters and my mother gave me valuable input; Victor Wortman, Joanne Baker, and Bob Fox supplied me with books; Jeremy Block, Anthony Block, and Phyllis Nugent opened doors for me, as have Peter Beard, Peter Tunney, and John Heminway; Tessa Jordan, Christine Jordan, and Laura Bentley were insightful researchers and location scouts; Shane Boocock and Anie Villepontoux helped me get on the road; John Tripp helped me bring safari home; and Layson Fox had the sense to ensure I stayed on track.

The concept for the book became a reality thanks to the support and imagination of my publisher Gibbs Smith, Quay and Sharon Hays and Christopher Robbins. I also want to thank designer Dana Granoski, editorial director Peter Hoffman, editor Dana Stibor, literary agent Jim Fitzgerald and literary counselor Jonathon Kirsch for their contributions.

Finally (but always first), I'm grateful for my "pride," Alexandra and John, my children who enthusiastically shared, first- and second-hand, my adventures abroad and, less enthusiastically, tolerated my work at home. They have always been the best part of my safaris: traveling with them, they are the best safari companions; traveling without them, their welcoming hugs make coming home the best part of any voyage.

Bibi Jordan

preface In East Africa, back in 1955, I found a way of life that featured an escape into the past, into a seemingly endless, diverse, unspoiled landscape with evolutionary realities everywhere... realities that bring one back and down to earth to "the darkness that may be felt."

I was inspired by the most adventuresome, highly educated, eccentric, humorous, really quite daring people that I met, such as Karen Blixen, her brother Thomas Dinesen, Bror Blixen, Philip Percival, Denys Finch Hatton, Edward "Cape-to-Cairo" Grogan, Lord Delamere, J.A. Hunter, Elsbeth Huxley, HRH the Prince of Wales, Johnny Boise, Gilbert Colville, Daniel Pomerox, James Southerland, George Eastman, J.H. Patterson, Bunny Allen, and many others.

All those people got along with the Africans, and got along with them in the wildest and most isolated, daring circumstances in exhilarating harmony, described by Karen Blixen's Somali servant, Kamante, as being "like the black and white keys of a piano, how they are played and produce melodious verses."

The legacy of these legendary characters lives on in the succeeding generations that constitute today's safari crowd. Calvin Cottar, a fourth-generation professional hunter, still runs the old-style safaris in the Maasai Mara just like his great-grandfather, the first American White Hunter, Chas Cottar, who entertained the royal family in the 1920s; Tara Bonham still leads game treks on horseback in the shadow of Mount Kilimanjaro, as did her grandfather, J.A. Hunter, considered by many, including Denys Finch Hatton, to have been one of the most experienced of them all. And, in the Okavango Delta, Randall Moore transforms into reality the dream of King Leopold of Belgium, who fantasized of riding through herds of game on elephant-back.

The romance and nostalgia of the old days has been captured on the screen in movies like *Savage Splendor, King Solomon's Mines,* and *Mogambo.* But, for all those who seek real-life adventure and larger-than-life characters, the thrill of safari living is still waiting to be discovered ... in Africa ... and in this book.

Peter Beard

Hog Ranch, Kenya

introduction

Before I saw this book, I wouldn't have been confident "safari" and "chic" were to be uttered in the same breath. Words as radiant as these have become belabored by overuse, pretension, linguistic indolence. There was a time when everything new—gold swizzle sticks, vinyl skirts, Hilton Head—were dubbed "chic."

Concurrently, the word safari had become a flaccid metaphor for any hint of motion—a hitchhike to Mombasa; a journey by motor coach to Tree Tops; an afternoon at Disney World, stir-fried by the body heat of strangers.

Those of us who are umbilically attached to Africa and who view its riddles, tragedy, loneliness, and generosity as private gifts for old souls might wince to learn that anything as perfect as the "true" safari can be reduced to a matter of style.

I now know that had I stuck to my guns, I would have been blind to a new adventure. Bibi Jordan has happened upon a creative phenomenon perfectly described by the title of this book. She celebrates a flair for life once hobbled by colonial banalities and hotel-chain convention. She has nailed her discovery into one elegantly accurate sound bite: *Safari Chic.*

About 15 years ago, something happened in Africa. Camps and lodges germinated upon ground formerly snubbed by those who had their eyes focused on the bottom line. The new innkeepers were inspired by different passions. One was to showcase the subtleties of their African obsession. Another was to let architecture assume the shape of their own lives—free-form, serendipitous, pregnant with paradox.

The creators of these lodges and camps have reassigned a new locus to luxury. They understand that Africa should be brought indoors, and that in doing so, this big-breasted land provides comforts hitherto unknown. *Chic* should be about appropriateness, about ingenious design, spontaneous surprise, and the accurate measure of human wants, altogether innocent of pretense.

I can recall my first discovery that African hospitality had reached new plateaus. Several years ago, I arrived at a very small private lodge, all wood and stone, owned by people who had never previously been hoteliers. Unwittingly, they had dismissed traditional assumptions of the hospitality industry. The architecture of this lodge contained few straight lines or squares. The pool clung precariously to a cliff above a herd of elephants. In my room, the large bed was designed to be a focus for sounds of the night. All that would separate me from Africa would be a thin mosquito net. Instead of imported chocolates on pillows, there were thoughtful gifts scattered everywhere—homemade soap, potpourri from dried flowers, nuts picked by a man carrying a spear. The bathroom, while absolutely private, was innocent of a door and the view from the tub was of a grazing kudu. Fireplaces were located where they were needed, walls removed wherever superfluous. As a consequence, Africa blew in from all directions. I sat above a million-mile view and tried to recall a line from Karen Blixen: "This is the place I was meant to be."

I have spent much of my life learning from Africa, and now I learn again: What I had believed to be a sometime thing—a brief moment of inspired African design—I now discover to be a creative current coursing the length of Africa's Great Rift. Africa has produced a very modern and distinctive style of its own. To enjoy it is to appreciate intimately why Africa, its people, its wildlife, its wild lands are so alive, so vital, so universal, and, in the end, so chillingly familiar to us all.

John Heminway

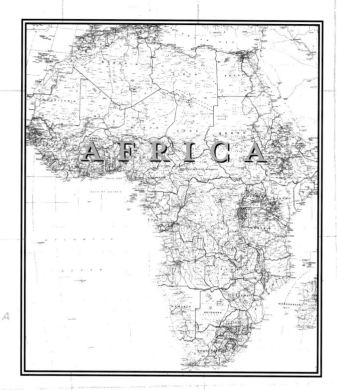

CONTENTS

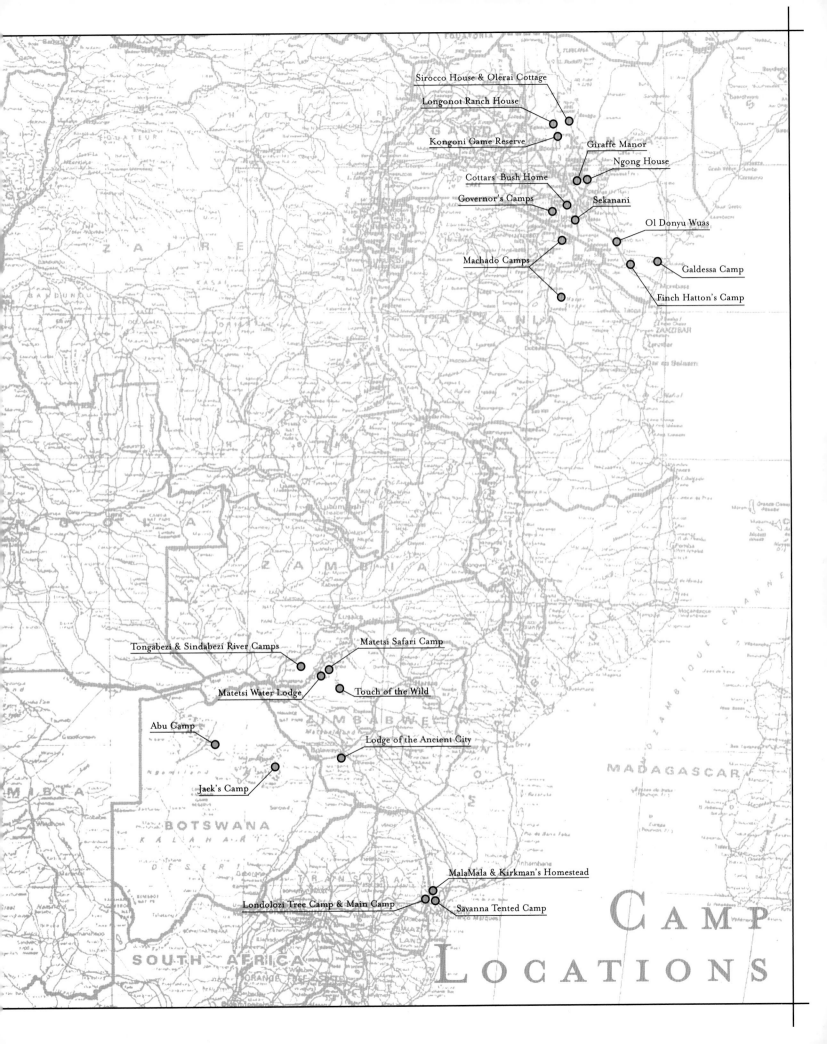

Sirocco House & Olerai Cottage

Longonot Ranch House

Kongoni Game Reserve

Giraffe Manor

Ngong House

Cottars' Bush Home

Governor's Camps

Sekanani

Ol Donyu Wuas

Machado Camps

Galdessa Camp

Finch Hatton's Camp

Tongabezi & Sindabezi River Camps

Matetsi Safari Camp

Matetsi Water Lodge

Touch of the Wild

Abu Camp

Lodge of the Ancient City

Jack's Camp

MalaMala & Kirkman's Homestead

Londolozi Tree Camp & Main Camp

Savanna Tented Camp

CAMP

LOCATIONS

On safari:
a telling definition

The glow of the sun setting over the Maasai Mara (upper right); the gleam of a lioness prowling in the Sabi Sands (lower right); the symmetry of zebra grazing in the Serengeti—these are the archetypal African scenes that await safari travelers.

*S*afari is a word packed with romance and adventure, conjuring up images of migrating herds and snow-capped mountains; sounds of thundering waterfalls and invisible predators; smells of campfires and canvas; feelings of camaraderie and fear.

Safari. It's a word that always leads to one destination: Africa, shrouded with mystery and magic, cradle of civilization and of mankind, that powerful mother-continent to us all.

Retracing the original derivation of the term is like analyzing Freudian word associations. I page through my

SAFARI.

THEODORE ROOSEVELT POPULARIZED IT;

ERNEST HEMINGWAY FICTIONALIZED IT;

KAREN BLIXEN ROMANTICIZED IT. IT IS A

TROPHY EVERYONE WANTS TO CAPTURE

ONCE IN A LIFETIME.

*"If there were one more thing I could do,
it would be to go on safari once again."*

—KAREN BLIXEN, IN HER FINAL LETTER

"*A voyage to a destination,
wherever it may be,
is also a voyage inside oneself.*"

—Laurens van der Post, *Venture to the Interior*

Arabic dictionary, remembering that Arabic words are not listed alphabetically. Instead, I must decipher three primary consonants which regroup into a progression of verb variations that, like minor and major keys on a scale, change the tone of the word.

Under the basic verb root, s-f-r, I find the following derived verbs:

1. Sa-fa-ra: to remove the veil
2. Sa-ffa-ra: to uncover, to discover
3. Saa-fa-ra: to go on a journey
4. As-fa-ra: to shine or glow with an aurora
5. Tasa-fa-ra: to rise, disappear into dust, clouds, sunset

On safari, I realized how apropos the definitions were. At dawn, I lifted a veil of mosquito netting off the bed, discovering the African bush bathed in the pink rays of dawn. Gulping down hot coffee served on a pewter tray, I set off on a journey—a game drive, walk, or boat ride. Each consecutive game sighting was like a miracle, filling me with joy and wonder. At day's end, sitting around a smoldering campfire and sipping

Elephants still tramp trails through the bush like those followed by early explorers who were led by Bushmen guides. Intuitive naturalists, the Bushmen now guide a new generation of trailblazers at Jack's Camp in Botswana (left).

The same landmarks and the same campsites that explorers used—like an ancient baobab tree at Kenya's Tsavo West National Park (above) or Goliath Safari's Mana Pools fly-camp in Zimbabwe (lower left)—are stepping stones on a journey to discover the beauty of African wildlife and culture.

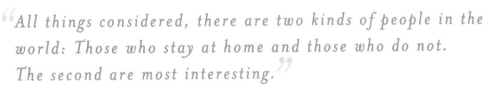

"All things considered, there are two kinds of people in the world: Those who stay at home and those who do not. The second are most interesting."

—RUDYARD KIPLING

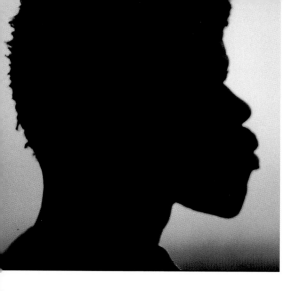

sundowners, I watched the sun sink into the horizon and then turned to see the moon rise in the dark African night.

Once back home, I wondered whether safari is just a metaphor for life. As the Japanese poet Basho wrote, "The journey is life and home is the destination." We are unveiled at birth and embark on the journey of life. As life experiences forge character into our personalities, we radiate our

The dramatic beauty of African sunsets, captured (opposite page) sinking into Botswana's Chobe River, gave rise to the safari custom of sundowners—chilled cocktails downed as the sun slips below the horizon.

Safari memories radiate with insights gained from encountering the timeless wisdom of the San Bushmen of the Kalahari (upper left) or the colorful customs of the Maasai warriors of the Mara/Serengeti plains (lower left and above).

Our untrained eyes will
never spot all the eyes
trained on us: Lazing in the
tree canopy or resting in the
savanna grasses, lions are so
well camouflaged that we
may pass by unaware of
their presence.

The expressive faces of
lions, especially cubs, make
it easy to attribute to them
human emotions such as
pride and friendliness, but
their wild instincts must
always be respected.

own individuality until we, too, disappear into a cloud of dust.

While on safari, I was impressed by how even in the bush, the safari set were *chic* in the French sense of the word—elegant, smart, with a certain savoir faire—the knack of handling everything "just right." The idea for this book came when, on the eve of departing on safari, I was asked to pick up and bring over 20 place settings from the Pottery Barn, 12 crystal glasses from Crate & Barrel, and five lamps from Restoration Hardware for the finishing touches of a new, ultra-exclusive camp.

When I arrived, I was amazed at how well the American merchandise complemented the camp's stunning interiors, a look that could easily be duplicated at home. I hope this book (a-sa-faa-r: also a derivative of s-f-r) unveils for you the *chic* of *safari* as we journey through Africa to discover its intoxicating beauty, ethnic tradition, and irresistible lure—freedom, nature, and a style that can introduce a wild, free look into our tame interiors.

"All I wanted to do now was get back to Africa.
We had not left it yet, but when I would wake in the night,
I would lie, listening, homesick for it already."

—Ernest Hemingway, *The Green Hills of Africa*

The Golden
Age of Safari

Over the years, a distinctive ethic has evolved around *safari* that gradually defined a style and a subtlety of character that the French term *chic*. Established by the first European expeditions and refined by subsequent generations of hunters and safari aficionados, the ethic was based on the tradition of the good-sporting, gentlemanly behavior of the British military command. The adventurers who first penetrated the African interior were intrepid British officers of the East India Company, who were out for "a bit of sport," in contrast to the early Dutch settlers or the later Victorian explorers.

Ironically, it was the wayward behavior of a young lady that set the wheels in motion for the first African safari. Lucia Green set sail from England for the island of St. Helena to marry her fiancé, William Burchell, but fell in love and instead married the ship's captain.[1] A crushed Burchell quit his job as a botanist for the East India Company and, lured by travelers' tales of Africa, sailed to Cape Town in 1810 to mend his broken heart.

In Cape Town, Burchell was astonished by the incredible biodiversity and decided to undertake an expedition into the interior to collect new specimens. He hired some Hottentot guides and purchased a Dutch Cape wagon.

Employing an early version of independent suspension, the Cape wagon was better engineered and stronger than the American prairie wagon. They were designed to be disassembled for portage across mountains and rivers and were the first collapsible equipment designed specifically for African journeys.

The mysterious waterscape created by Zimbabwe's man-made Lake Kariba (above) stirs primal feelings of desolation and wonder similar to those experienced by the first safari travelers.

In charge of the Black Rhino Project at Kenya's Tsavo East National Park, Oliver Mnyambo (above) is representative of the Africans' awareness that game conservation is key to the development of national economies.

Never having slept one night out-doors, Burchell set out on 19 June, 1811 and for four years slept either on the ground or in his wagon. During his expedition he traveled 4,500 miles, collected 40,000 botanical specimens, made 500 drawings, and discovered four species of animals.

This first safari, which, ironically, eschewed game kill to focus on plant life, became the forerunner of the Great African Game Safaris. Burchell's travelogue, *Travels in the Interior of Southern Africa*, fired up the imagination of another English officer of the East India Company, Cornwallis Harris, who resolved to follow Burchell's footsteps—but with

Like Machado Safari's Swala Camp in Tanzania's Tarangire National Park (left), the campsites of the 1800s were home to wild animals in addition to safari travelers. Two impala buck graze at dawn, oblivious to a hungry lioness stalking them nearby.

"*Nothing but breathing the air of Africa, and actually walking through it, can communicate the indescribable sensations.*"

—WILLIAM BURCHELL

the aim of amassing animal, not plant, species.

An experienced hunter from his youth in England and his army career in India, Harris arrived with his camping provisions, including his teapot, tent, drawing materials, and gunpowder. The first traveler able to contrast African safari life with Indian, he found Africa much more challenging than the lavish Indian *shikars,* elaborate staged hunts for

sportsmen traveling in *howdahs* on trained elephants, accompanied by armies of specialized servants and accommodated in ornate oriental tents.

But he made himself comfortable with a routine that still rules safaris today—waking before dawn to a strong cup of tea, leaving for a game-ride at sunrise, stopping for a hearty breakfast at mid-morning, continuing on until lunch at noon, and returning at

dusk for a gourmet dinner, followed by drinks and cigars around the campfire. Taking casts of the footprint of each species, he became an expert tracker. Never without his sketching supplies, which he stashed in his cap, he was the first European to document comparative animal behavior in Africa—as critical to the success of safaris today as in his time.

The first book on game hunting in Africa, Cornwallis Harris' *The Wild Sports of Southern Africa*, was so popular that it was reprinted five times. Explorers such as Dr. David Livingstone, Samuel Baker, Richard Francis Burton, James Grant, and John Speke used the book to prepare for their own expeditions. For numerous sportsmen, raised in the British tradition of the hunt and the Empire and retaining a schoolboy romance with wildlife, Harris' book offered an irresistible escape from the confines of Victorian society.

"We were all bitten in those days by Captain Harris," wrote William Cotton Oswell, who embarked on his first safari with his friend Mungo Murray in 1844. A legendary personality even in his formative years, Oswell served as the model for the Brooke brothers, the quintessential British schoolboys in Thomas Hughes' classic *Tom Brown's School Days*. In Africa he became the first true European safari guide, teaching Livingstone how to survive in the bush and accompanying the competitive explorer Samuel Baker and Florence, his future wife, whom he had bought for seven pounds sterling at a Hungarian slave auction.

Oswell made two trips with Livingstone, accompanying him across the Kalahari Desert to discover Lake Ngami and along the Zambezi River to the Upper Zambezi. Livingstone, Oswell realized, was a poor shot and a worse mount—the missionary rode a bad-tempered ox that relished brushing him against low branches and then kicked him when he fell. Despite his substantial contribution to Livingstone's explorations, Oswell, displaying an innate selflessness that characterizes the best of guides, conceded all

Today's luxury safari camps would have satisfied Burchell, who found African safaris more challenging than the lavish Indian *shikars*—staged events for hunters traveling in howdahs on elephant-back and accommodated in ornate tents.

Having studied Livingstone's *Missionary Travels*, Selous set off at 19 for South Africa. But, by the 1870s, the big game had been decimated in much of southern Africa and the best elephant hunting was in the northeast, where the tsetse fly kept horse and hunter at bay. Selous, accompanied by an experienced Hottentot tracker, Cigar, was not daunted—setting off on foot, they began the tradition of the walking safari.

Tutored by Cigar, Selous became a superlative tracker much in demand as a paid safari guide and was hired by imperialist Cecil Rhodes to lead the pioneer expedition that settled Rhodesia, now known as Zimbabwe. Like Oswell and Livingstone, Selous admired the Bushmen, whom he considered to be the best naturalists and trackers. Selous himself became renowned for his astute field observations, recorded in four books.

One of his greatest admirers was President Theodore Roosevelt, who edited some of his chapters and in 1903 invited him to the White House, where the two men went rock climbing, horse riding, and river racing in the Potomac during the day and spun hunting tales in the White House during the evening.

"There was never a more welcome guest at the White House than Frederick Selous," Roosevelt commented. When Roosevelt embarked

the glory of these discoveries to Livingstone.

Both Oswell and Livingstone had a high regard for the Bushmen of the Kalahari. Although there was no running water in the desert and very little in wells, their guide Ramotobi showed them how the Bushmen bore drinking holes into underground water systems and dug for basketball-sized tubers that contained a cool fluid. Traveling slowly with his pregnant wife, Mary, Livingstone and his party were able to cross the desert and discover the extraordinary wildlife of

Lake Ngami and the adjoining Okavango Delta, which is still considered the Eden of Africa.

Back in England, at Oswell's renowned alma mater, Rugby, young Frederick Courtenay Selous was gaining a reputation. Repeated transgressions—run-ins with the gamekeeper and nocturnal escapades in the forest—caused Selous to be sent to the headmaster, who recognized the same traits Oswell had displayed. Asking him what his objective was, the lad answered, "I mean to be like a Livingstone."

on safari, Selous was chosen to coordinate the trip that marked the start of luxurious safaris for wealthy American clients, a development that was to sustain the safari business for decades.

By the time Roosevelt left the White House, he was recognized as a leading conservationist and had become the spokesperson for the environmental movement in the United States. But Roosevelt was also an avid hunter. Heading for Kenya, Roosevelt immensely enjoyed his trip and collected specimens for the Smithsonian. He relished the camp life, which seemed extravagantly luxurious compared to Western camping, although it was considered rather austere by some of the safari professionals. He was especially impressed with the Maasai warriors, the moran, "as graceful and sinewy as panthers." Although the landscape reminded Roosevelt of the West, the lifestyle was just like the novels of one of his favorite authors, H. Rider Haggard.

As a young man, Haggard had spent six years in South Africa in the 1860s, when Selous was making his name. Enamored with the Zulu and the land even more than the game, Haggard faithfully kept a diary. After returning to England, his brother dared him to write a book of his real-life escapades as exciting as the newly released Robert Louis Stevenson

fictional adventure *Treasure Island*. Drawing on his memories of Selous, Zulu friends, and the breathtaking landscape, Haggard dashed off *King Solomon's Mines* in six weeks. In the first year, it went through 13 editions in the States alone and, translated into 19 languages, the book has never been out of print.

Dedicated to "big and little boys," the book had many fans, including Theodore Roosevelt, Winston Churchill, D.H. Lawrence, C.S. Lewis, Henry Miller, Graham Greene, and Rudyard Kipling.

Lunching with Haggard at the White House before he went on safari, Roosevelt commented, "It is an odd thing that you and I, brought up in different countries and following such different pursuits, should have identical ideas and aims."

The president's enthusiasm also inspired another author-in-the-making. Dressed in a copy of the famous khakis designed for the presidential safari by outfitter Willis & Geiger, young Ernest Hemingway often visited the African animal exhibits at Chicago's Field Museum of

LIKE ROOSEVELT AND HEMINGWAY, TODAY'S TRAVELERS
FLOCK TO AFRICA TO SHOOT THE KING OF THE ANIMALS—
BUT WITH CAMERAS RATHER THAN RIFLES.

Natural History, fantasizing that he was Roosevelt in Kenya. At 24, Hemingway went on safari with the same professional hunter who had escorted Roosevelt, Philip Percival. The trip became the basis for a book, *The Green Hills of Africa,* and two short stories, "The Snows of Kilimanjaro" and "The Short Happy Life of Francis Macomber," whose main character was partially based on Percival. Toward the end of his life, Hemingway, armed with a spear and dressed in ochre-dyed clothes like those of the Maasai, went on safari once more with the man he most admired, Percival.

With public attention focused on safaris—real and fictional—it did not take Hollywood long to get in on the act. An early film version of *King Solomon's Mines*, filmed mainly in England, received mixed reviews. But the chief gaffer was a fan of Haggard and when he became a top MGM

Warmed by the early morning sunshine, a pride of lions settle down to a long day's rest in the Sabi Sands. Lovers of night, lions are best tracked before dawn or after nightfall, which is permitted only in a few locations, including South Africa's Sabi Sands Private Game Reserve (below).

producer, Sam Zimbalist mounted the biggest safari since Roosevelt's to film a new version starring Deborah Kerr and Stewart Granger.

Traveling 14,000 miles on safari over a five-month period, the film employed 53 filmmakers, more than 100 Africans, 80 servants, and four professional hunters. Released in 1950, the film was an immediate success, winning an Academy Award for Best Color Cinematography.

The safari professionals had earned the respect of MGM and in 1952 director John Ford set off on an even bigger filmmaking safari to produce *Mogambo*, starring Ava Gardner, Grace Kelly, and Clark Gable. Outfitted like Roosevelt and Hemingway in Willis & Geiger's bush gear, Clark Gable was transformed from a Hollywood hero into a real bush hero by saving a crew member from the jaws of a crocodile.

About 30 years later, Universal Studios embarked on the biggest filmmaking safari, costing nearly $30 million and employing 10,000 actors. Starring Meryl Streep and Robert Redford, *Out of Africa* projected an idealized image of safari life and the settler movement in East Africa.

By the end of the century, the reality of history and the fantasy of Hollywood had created a "safari chic." Guides were expected to have the smooth charm and steady nerve of the dashing young officers of the British India Company and the professional hunters that followed them. They displayed a respectful appreciation of everything Africa had to offer: the game, the culture, and the bush. The safaris they organized were run with paramilitary precision and a standard of elegance, romance, and adventure that the world had learned to expect from travel journals, literature, and movies.

The
Quintessential
Fly-Camp

*One of Kenya's best professional
hunters, Peter Behr (above),
apprenticed with Glen Cottar,
the grandson of the first
American White Hunter.*

Though the concept of safari and Great White Hunters was romanticized by Haggard, Hemingway, and Hollywood, more often than not, the professional hunters were ordinary settler farmers who shot well. Their sights were set on earning extra income rather than accumulating hunting trophies.

Like the etymology of *safari*, the phrase *White Hunter* has an interesting origin that traces back to Lord Delamere, the leader of the turn-of-the-century settler movement in Kenya. Requiring two hunters, Lord Delamere recruited a Somali camp headman and a young hunter named Alan Black. To avoid the inevitable confusion caused by Black's surname, Delamere referred to the Somali as the "black hunter" and to Black as the "white hunter."[1] The nickname stuck and the phrase *White Hunter* became part of the safari vernacular.

Today, safari clients shoot photos, not game, yet the skills of the White Hunter are still in demand. First, the elegance and style of the quintessential fly-camps are as appealing today as they were a century ago. Second, only a skilled hunter can safely lead clients on the ultimate safari—a walk through the African wilderness. Finally, the ability of a professional hunter to interpret nature, recognize tracks, and transform a still landscape into one teeming with animals is essential for a successful safari. Fortunately, the legacy of the Golden Age of Safari can still be experienced at exquisite camps run by the sons and grandsons of the Great White Hunters.

All the romance and seduction of safari life comes alive in old-style camps, where the day begins with a morning game walk accompanied by a professional hunter and culminates with sundowners served at makeshift bush bars.

"*There is something about safari life that makes you forget all your sorrows and feel as if you had drunk half a bottle of champagne—bubbling over with heartfelt gratitude for being alive.*"

—KAREN BLIXEN

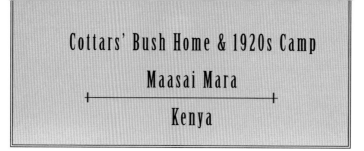

the roaring '20s

The Maasai Mara is home to Africa's longest continuously operating safari ventures, founded by the first American White Hunter, Chas Cottar. After taking his family across Texas, Oklahoma, and Colorado in a covered wagon, he was inspired by headline stories of President Roosevelt's safari to move his family from Cedar County, Oklahoma, to Nairobi, Kenya.

From 1909 to 1941, Chas Cottar and his sons, Mike, Bud, and Ted, contributed to the romantic image of safari with wild nonconformist cowboy ways—they introduced motorized safaris and photo safaris to Kenya. In 1924, when the Duke and Duchess of York, the future King Edward VIII, and the Queen Mother traveled to Kenya, the Cottar family provided the guiding services just as they continue to guide the elite today.

As Glen Cottar and his wife did, Lou and Peter Behr (below) welcome to the Cottars' exclusive hideaway guests who want to experience the Mara in complete privacy and seclusion.

The youngest professional hunter ever licensed in Kenya, Peter, who was raised and trained by the Cottars, explained that the secret of spotting game is "not to look for the shape of the whole animal, but for something that perhaps doesn't fit in—perhaps a substance too solid for a leaf or shadow—then you might identify the outline of the backbone crawling along a branch or a criss-crossed paw."

THE PARAMILITARY OPERATION OF TRANSPORTING THE CAMP IS COORDINATED FROM THE COTTARS' BUSH HOME OFFICE (RIGHT). CROSSING STREAMS AND INTERSECTING HERDS OF GAME, THE TRUCKS ARRIVE ONE DAY IN ADVANCE OF CLIENTS. OVERNIGHT, TENTS ARE ERECTED, FOUR-POSTER BEDS CONSTRUCTED, CANVAS BATHS UNFOLDED, SHOWERS HOISTED, AND DROP-TOILETS DUG. BY THE TIME GUESTS ARRIVE, SAFARI CHAIRS ARE READIED, DRINKS ARE CHILLED, AND CLASSIC MUSIC WAFTS THROUGH THE SAVANNA AIR.

At the Cottar family Bush Home, built by Chas' grandson Glen, and Cottar's Camp, operated by Chas' great-grandson Calvin, today's travelers experience the romance and mystique of bygone times. Cottar's Camp is the re-creation of the quintessential fly-camps where Chas Cottar entertained clients in the Roaring '20s. Packed into a vast accumulation of trunks are tents, mosquito nets, heirloom antiques, cases of champagne, fresh fruits and vegetables, tinned provisions, and all the necessities for luxury in the bush. Whereas in the past, Calvin's great-grandfather distributed these items in 60-pound "head-loads" to 30 porters per hunter and 50 porters per client, Calvin simply loads the supplies onto

three enormous four-wheel-drive lorries.

Oblivious to the behind-the-scenes operation, I was taken on a game walk by guide Peter Behr, who learned his art from Glen Cottar. Stopping at a stream to wash our hands, Peter pointed to fresh leopard tracks in the riverbed and then identified a light drag mark in the mud. Minuscule smears of blood on a thorny bush provided more evidence. "The leopard pulled its prey upstream to wash away the scent," he said, pointing to smaller, doglike tracks "that had already attracted a pack of hyena."

Scanning the landscape for the leopard's lair, Peter pointed to a distant tree whose lichen-spotted trunk was itself as dappled as the leopard's coat. Even with binoculars, it was barely possible to identify the leopard that Peter had seen with bare eyes. Armed with instincts refined by four generations of bush lore and confirmed by a professional hunter's certification, Peter bagged for me the ultimate safari adventure—stalking game on foot.

The master tent is a study of purity of line and form (left and right). The collapsible four-poster bed is dressed in dreamy layers of lace, mosquito netting, and embroidered linen. After adrenaline-pumping game walks, the bedroom needs to be reassuring—and it is.

HER MAJESTY HAS THE HAPPIEST MEMORIES OF HER VISIT IN 1924, PARTICULARLY THE TIME ON SAFARI WHEN MR. COTTAR WAS WITH THE DUKE OF YORK.

—QUEEN ELIZABETH, IN A LETTER TO THE COTTAR FAMILY

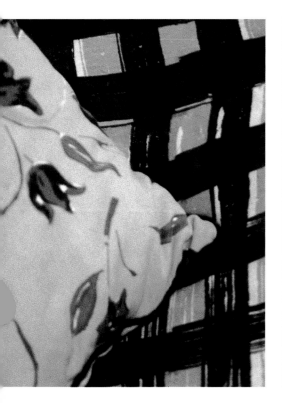

Linens in bright hues reflect the colors of Maasai jewelry (far left). A turn-of-the-century wardrobe trunk converts to a lady's dressing chest of drawers (left). Once guests depart, the bedroom is disassembled and packed into the trunk for transport back home.

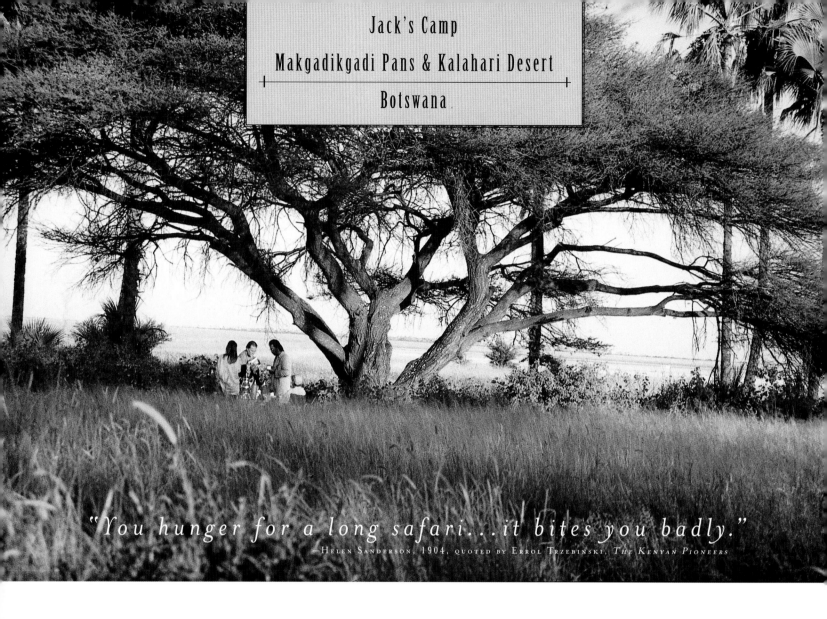

"You hunger for a long safari...it bites you badly."
—HELEN SANDERSON, 1904, QUOTED BY ERROL TRZEBINSKI, *THE KENYAN PIONEERS*

one in the bush

One of the hottest safari destinations is Botswana, where privileged safari clients track with mankind's oldest hunters, the San Bushmen of the Kalahari at the Bousfield family's camp, Jack's Camp.

Jack's Camp is named after the infamous Jack Bousfield, a professional hunter and notorious crocodile hunter mentioned in the *Guinness Book of Animal Records*, whose family headed the Game Department in Tanganyika, had several species named after them, relocated the last Arabian oryx, and trained the lion stars of *Born Free*.

Jack traveled throughout southern Africa, developing a reputation as one of the best trackers. His family joined him frequently as he traveled into the remotest bush in search of the savage beauty of the uncharted

Africa of his childhood. His son, Ralph, remembers as a child sleeping in a bedroll under the stars and waking to the sensation of warm, humid breath on his cheek—a lion.

"I let out the loudest string of expletives anyone's heard in the bush," Ralph recalls. "The lion vanished, but lions rarely attack anyone under a white sheet or white mosquito netting, anyway."

On a tracking expedition in Botswana, Jack stumbled on a setting so stunning that he immediately envisaged a new, innovative safari: using four-wheel-drive quad-bikes, guests would explore a hitherto unknown and impenetrable area in an ecologically sensitive manner. After Jack's death, Ralph pursued his vision, establishing Jack's Camp in the Makgadikgadi Pans.

A relic of one of Earth's largest superlakes, the Makgadikgadi is an endless vista of grasslands about the size of Switzerland. One of Africa's most important wetland sites, in the rainy season the pans fill with summer showers, attracting flamingo, waterbirds, and a migration of tens of thousands of wildebeest and zebra with predators following in their wake.

Flying out to Jack's Camp in a small bush plane, I looked down onto a vast unbroken expanse of savanna, the surface dotted with hundreds of puffs of dust that looked like little genies bursting from the confines of the earth. Drawing closer, I could distinguish thousands of zebra stampeding to escape the drone of the aircraft. While migrations occur elsewhere in Africa, here the open grasslands and absence of tree cover present a view of biblical proportions.

The pilot pointed to a tree so enormous that even from the air I could recognize its primitive profile. Looking like a toddler's drawing of a tree, this ancient baobab serves as a beacon for camp guests, just as it did for explorers like Livingstone, who camped within its outstretched branches and carved their initials on the fibrous bark.

Ralph Bousfield (opposite page, lower left) greets guests for a mid-morning brunch under the acacia tree (opposite page, top). Game walks are conducted by Cobra, a San Bushman (top). A hartebeest skull crowns Main Camp (above). Gas lanterns are readied for the evening (left).

The plane bounced to a stop on a landing strip cut into the grassland, where a shiny green Land Rover awaited to take us to camp. After settling in, we gathered under the umbrellalike acacia tree, where we were introduced to the guides. Like a lost tribe of debonair desert desperadoes—part boffin, part adventurer, and part Hemingway—the guides at Jack's Camp are unique, providing insight into the Kalahari that supports the greatest diversity of wildlife found in any desert.

Most impressive of the guides is Cobra. Dressed in a guest's discarded shirt and tattered hat, the dignity of his broad brow and topaz eyes had passed unnoticed. But in the buckskin loincloth of a San Bushman with a bow and arrow slung on his shoulder, he looks as noble as a black-maned Kalahari lion.

Words crackled like sparks as he spoke the !Xo click language. Cobra

pointed to tracks too tiny to be easily distinguishable. "Tortoise," our Motswana guide, Super, translated. "San learn to track before they walk: Babies are given a tortoise to play with and, crawling after it in the soft sand, they quickly learn to recognize its tracks. Then, when they're older, they can always find a snuffbox when they need one," he said with a laugh,

fingering a beaded tortoise shell hanging from his neck.

At nightfall, spinning yarns around a campfire, we paused to hear distant howls. "A jackal," Cobra stated, "on the track of a lion." He can distinguish the call of jackals maintaining contact with the pack, a long, smooth, diminishing howl, from its cry on the track of a

predator, a shuddering howl that diminishes with a soft cough, which, when repeated, means it is following a lion.

The next morning, straddling quad-bikes in convoy with a supply truck, we set off for a three-night camping trip on Kudu Island, a granite extrusion island studded with baobabs, where there are still

"'MAKGADIKGADI?' I ASKED WHAT WAS OUT THERE,
AND THEY SAID, 'NOTHING—ONLY IDIOTS GO THERE.'
I THOUGHT, FINE, THAT'S THE PLACE FOR ME."

—JACK BOUSFIELD

places no human foot has trod. But first we detour to check Cobra's hypothesis. Heading toward circling vultures, we find hyena feasting on a fresh zebra kill.

Pulling out his knife, Cobra hacked off the zebra tail. "A new fly-swatter," he said, grinning. He cut a thin slice from the exposed esophagus of the zebra and slid it onto the shaft of his spear. "To avoid the wood from splitting," he explained.

Interestingly, like the Great White Hunters, San hunters balance resourcefulness, humility, and tact. After a series of kills, for example, a successful hunter will refrain from participating so that others can reciprocate: A hunter's tally might be appreciated up to a point, but too much success would cause envy and discord.[2]

Here in the Kalahari, a culture as old as the San and as contemporary as quad-bikers share the safari ethic. Unexpectedly, in one of the last great wilderness areas, one of the last great luxuries of life can be experienced: the seductive charm, the elegant service, and raw adventure of the quintessential fly-camp of the African safari.

Hunter Homesteads

The early settlers shared with the White Hunters a love of adventure and an addiction to freedom. Settler women, in fact, became as legendary as the White Hunters. Long before the catchphrase was invented, settler women were liberated females.

For example, in 1910 Cara Buxton walked from Cairo to Nairobi. "I'm so happy in a tent, I don't much care if the house is never finished," she wrote back home to England. "Great excitement last night—a lion came and frightened us and bit one of my donkeys very badly."[1]

More often, young women sailed to Mombasa, engaged to fiancés who had traveled on ahead, sometimes years in advance. Upon arrival, they were quickly wed to avoid scandal and departed on the long journey to the Kenyan highlands, where the colonial government offered land grants.

To many a bride's surprise, setting up home in the highlands meant settling for paraffin crates for furniture, gunnysacking for curtains, and empty paraffin tins for stoves, coolers, water carriers, jelly molds, roasting tins, and roof tiles. The women learned to make soap from zebra fat and bottle brushes from warthog bristles. They learned from the Maasai how to make poultices out of dung and how to close wounds with thorns. Dried impala hooves became ashtrays and antlers became cloth racks.

Newcomers soon realized that one of the most important skills was a hospitality that became as synonymous with settler life as the Big Five—the lion, the leopard, the elephant, the Cape buffalo, and the rhinoceros—did with the White Hunters' lifestyle. Travelers asked for little more than a roof over their heads and a simple meal, but they provided something much more valuable: news.

Succeeding generations of settler families still offer travelers the legendary hospitality of the bush. Today, homesteads in the highlands of Kenya and the lowveld of South Africa retain the cozy warmth and eccentric character of bygone days. Meals are no longer cooked in a stove fashioned from a paraffin tin, but the freshness of the food, the lavishness of the menus, and the conviviality of the hosts remain unchanged.

"EVERYTHING THAT YOU SAW MADE FOR GREATNESS AND FREEDOM AND UNEQUALED NOBILITY," WROTE KAREN BLIXEN. JUST THE KNOWLEDGE THAT GAME WAS BEYOND THE FARM GATE GAVE "A SHINE AND PLAY TO THE ATMOSPHERE."

The daily struggle to inject some civilization into an unpredictable environment shaped the eccentric character of the settlers still retained at homesteads like Giraffe Manor (left) and Kongoni Game Reserve.

millionaire homestead

In the 1900s, wealthy single women often married into the families of impoverished European nobility. The story of Karen Blixen is well known: Her father was a prosperous Danish military officer who had worked as a fur trader in the United States and lived with the Indians, developing an admiration of them as his daughter did with the Africans. Karen longed to go to Africa with her beloved Swedish cousin, but since her affection wasn't reciprocated, she married his twin brother instead. Bror Blixen-Finecke owned nothing more than the family title Baron, so the bride's family gave the couple a coffee plantation in Kenya—which became the inspiration for Karen Blixen's book *Out of Africa*, written under her *nome de plume*, Isak Dinesen.[2]

Now a museum, Karen Blixen's wedding present can't be booked for a night, but Countess de Perigny's can. Born in 1877 to a Pittsburgh railroad millionaire, 21-year-old

The logo and name for the farm that Countess de Perigny built in 1926 are derived from the unusual flat-headed antelope, kongoni; they thrive in the Kenyan highlands.

Karen Blixen's brick farmhouse (left) is representative of the architecture of the old hunter homesteads. A table fashioned from an old millstone from India served as her desk on staff paydays.

The grave of the Countess de Perigny (top) at Kongoni Game Reserve overlooks Lake Naivasha. Today, Gianna and Bruno Brighetti (above) welcome guests to join their family and share the settler heritage.

Margaret Thaw married George Lauder Carnegie, nephew of the steel magnate-philanthropist. After her husband died, she married into the French nobility, becoming the Countess de Perigny.

Originally built for the Countess, Kongoni Game Reserve is now the home of the Brighetti family. Like the Count de Perigny, Bruno Brighetti brought his young bride, Gianna Bellinger Zasio, daughter of an aristocratic Italian family, on honeymoon to Africa. She arrived with a trousseau of 17 monogrammed trunks, which for the first year of their marriage accompanied them on safari. True to Gianna's upbringing, whenever they made camp, they set the "table"— a trunk—with a linen tablecloth, silver cutlery, and pewter candlesticks. When Gianna became pregnant, they bought the Kongoni Farm and developed it into a private game reserve.

Now at dinner, Gianna presides over a formal candlelit table of gourmet Italian food. "The Big Five at Kongoni means Parmesan cheese, olive oil, capers, risotto, and pasta" is Gianna's motto. After cognac in the game room, I retired to find a hot-water bottle in the bed and a copy of Dante's poems to my namesake, Beatrice, on my bedside table—a green trunk inscribed with the initials of Bruno Brighetti and Gianna Bellingeri Zasio.

Walking in the gardens the next day, I saw the marble tomb of the countess: her epitaph, "Always beautiful, always loving, always kind," seems as fitting for the estate's current owner as it was for the first one.

"THE PIONEERS' FARMS WERE MADE OF NOTHING AND EVERYTHING...HACKED OUT OF BUSH AND ROCKS, COAXED OUT OF NEW EARTH...THEY WERE MADE OF IGNORANCE AND INNOVATION, SHARP PRACTICE, SKILL, LUCK, DOGGED PERSISTENCE AND, BY NO MEANS LEAST, BY HUMOUR AND HEARTBREAK."

—ERROL TRZEBINSKI, *THE KENYAN PIONEERS*

Settler homes are filled with stories and memories. Heirloom silver from Italy adorns the patio dining table;
impala horns from the bush grace a bedside table; a brass coffee set from Zanzibar brightens the bathroom;
and a Koran stand from Lamu holds open the Brighetti family photo album.

a ride on the wild side

Hemingway's African stories regale with the thrill of safari life, but the home built for his fourth wife, Martha Gellhorn, is more reminiscent of an Adirondack camp than a Kilimanjaro tent. A trailblazer for female journalists, Martha found the site for her writer's retreat on the farm of Tubby Block, the son of Lithuanian Abraham Block, one of Kenya's most esteemed original settlers who rose from impoverished matzo factory worker to the founder of a chain of hotels, headed by Nairobi's prestigious Norfolk Hotel, still the traditional staging point for luxury safaris in Kenya.

Designed by Martha and built under Tubby's supervision, the home was nicknamed Casa Matata (Problem House) because of Martha's acrimonious temperament. The world's first woman war reporter, whose 50-year career spanned the Spanish Civil War

Longonot Ranch House
(*opposite page, top*) *is the base
for equestrian safaris led by
Tony Church and Maasai
guides* (*opposite page, bottom*). *"As a teenager growing
up on Athi Plains in Kenya,
the big sport was to round up
wildebeest on horseback and to
catch zebra by the tail at full
gallop. These adventures on
horseback amongst the game
inspired me to introduce horseback safaris," said Tony, whose
preference is for nomadic travel
in wilderness areas.*

After Hemingway's fourth wife, Martha Gellhorn, left Longonot in favor of her beach house in Mombasa, the Church family renovated Casa Matata, adding rooms but retaining the warm, colonial, ranch-style atmosphere.

"*There was the stillness of the eternal beginning, the world as it has always been.*"

—CARL JUNG, DESCRIBING THE ATHI PLAINS OF KENYA

to the recent Arab-Israeli wars, Martha's three marriages were fraught with tension. Even Hemingway she derided as being "one of the greatest self-created myths in history."

Casa Matata is now owned by Tony Church, who, with his son, Gordon, leads equestrian safaris through herds of zebra, impala, and giraffe and shares camps with lion, hyena, and baboon. "We cover about 200 miles a day, uninterrupted by fences, telegraph poles, or tarmac roads," Tony explained. "We canter with giraffe; we forge rivers full of hippos. Sure, there's the occasional confrontation with buffalo, elephant, and lion that provide a real thrill...but in 26 years we've never had a fatality."

"Of course, there are unpredictable turns in this part of the world—that's the beauty of Africa," Gordon added. "On our 'bimble in the bundu' (settler slang for a ride in the bush), the dust of Africa seeps into your body and a bond is reborn. I call it 'genetic memory' and it's one of the most powerful sensations you can ever experience.

"Like the Wild West, here in the saddle you buck the stress of everyday life, ride the adrenaline rush of a wildlife chase, and taste the passion for freedom that has always characterized settler life in Africa."

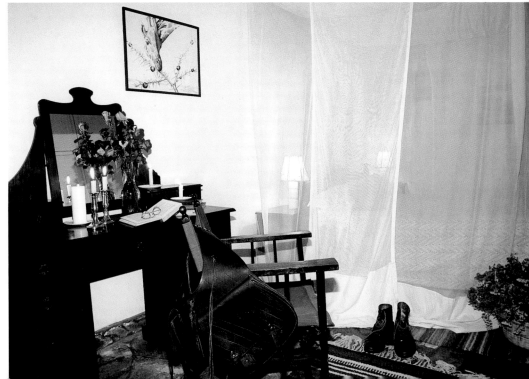

the green hunters

Also on Lake Naivasha is another literary home: Sirocco House, whose owners were the catalyst for the *Babar* books. To amuse her sons, Laurent and Mathieu, pianist Cecile de Brunhoff reinterpreted the African hunting tales told by her husband's cousin, Giselle, into bedtime stories—but from an orphaned elephant's point of view. Their father, artist Jean de Brunhoff, fighting a fatal case of tuberculosis, turned the stories into a book series about Babar the elephant. Losing his mother to a hunter's bullet, Babar is adopted by a kind old lady who, like Cecile, has a trim figure, plays the piano, and teaches her little ones the value of life.

Daughter of Philippe Bunau-Varilla, the engineer of the Panama Canal, Giselle and her husband, Mario Rocco, originally left Paris to live as artists in the United States but, disenchanted by bohemian life, Giselle returned to France, where a Belgian friend convinced her that a fortune could be made in Africa. After a shopping spree to outfit herself for the trip, her purchases were conveniently packed in 60 aluminum trunks. Summoning her husband from the States, the couple sailed to Dar es Salaam, boarded the train to Lake Tanganyika, and took a boat to Ujiji. There, at the location where Stanley located Livingstone in 1871, they found their Belgian friend,

hired 60 porters, and set off on foot on a yearlong elephant hunt in the Congo.

But Giselle and Mario found they preferred preserving elephants in paintings rather than killing them. When Giselle became pregnant, the young couple realized they needed to track down a hospital, not more elephants. From the Congo they walked to Lake Victoria and continued by boat and train to Nairobi, where their child was born.

While Giselle cared for the baby, Mario, a former World War I pilot, hired a plane to get the birth certificate signed by the Attorney General, who was fishing on a lake island in the Kenyan highlands. Engine failure

"The warmth and the culture of the Roccos made me feel welcome and at home, and I always looked forward to visiting them, for nothing obvious or boring could ever be found within their aura."

—Kuki Gallmann, *I Dreamed of Africa*

Olerai Cottage (opposite page), the original farmhouse that the Roccos built, has been augmented with several newer bungalows available to guests. Sirocco House (above), the Roccos' Art Deco house, can also be rented by visitors who want to step back into the elegance of 1920s safari life.

THE CAST TUSK OF ONE OF AFRICA'S MOST
REVERED ELEPHANTS ADORNS THE LIVING
ROOM (LEFT). ON "GREEN SAFARIS,"
CLIENTS ARE PRESENTED WITH A SIMILIAR
CAST OF THE TUSK OF AN ELEPHANT
THEY SPONSOR.

forced Mario to land on the mudflats of Lake Naivasha, where, serendipitously, an Irish mechanic rescued him and took him to his farm. By the time his plane was fixed, Mario had also fixed on a price for a home for himself, Giselle, and the new baby.

Sirocco House is now the home of their daughter, Oria, and her husband, Iain Douglas-Hamilton, who, in a twist of fate, are the world's most renowned elephant conservationists. The home is headquarters for their nonprofit Save the Elephants Foundation.

Although her parents came to Africa obsessed with ivory hunting, Oria and her husband have remained in Africa developing a new safari concept called "green hunting." With a scientific team, clients track a breeding herd and shoot an adult elephant with a tranquilizer dart. A GTS technology-equipped collar is then placed on the elephant, a "hunter's photo" is taken, and the tusk is cast for the client. Just as readers all over the world have followed the adventures of Babar, now a global network of computer users will be able to monitor the progress of breeding herds in Kenya as elephants once again repopulate the forests of Africa.

An extraordinary Art Deco creation, Sirocco House (above and below) was designed in the 1930s by French modernistic architect Herve Bazin.

In the guest bedroom, an ornate Lamu
bed is surrounded by murals depicting
the travels of Marco Polo painted by
Oria's father, artist Mario Rocco.

"Surrounded by family mementos of our
Afro–Franco–Italian heritage, guests
can relax in a private residence on the
grounds of a traditional farm where,
with the use of a car and a plane, they
can experience the Africa of my parents'
times in the 1920s," Oria explained.

a tall story

On the outskirts of Nairobi, travelers are welcomed at another magnificent family house to share in Jock Leslie-Melville's family legacy of conservation and literature. Jock's father was David Leslie-Melville, the Earl of Leven and Melville in Scotland. He met Jock's mother on board a ship sailing to Mombasa in 1919. Like Lucia Green, the protagonist of the first safari, she was travel-ing reluctantly to fulfill an arranged marriage contract, but fell in love with the earl and married him instead.

Born in Kenya, Jock and his sister spoke Swahili before English. Educated at Eton and Sandhurst, Jock returned to Kenya to take up Kenyan citizenship, working with Jomo Kenyatta for Uhuru, the Kenyan independence movement.

Built in 1932 by the "King of the Macintosh Toffees," South African David Duncan, Giraffe Manor became the home of Daisy, an endangered Rothschild giraffe, when Jock and Betty Leslie-Melville bought the estate in 1974. Although Daisy no longer lives there, her seven grandchildren and Betty's two grandsons now host guests from around the world.

Giraffe Manor looks like an old English country house— but it's set in primal forest, shared by giraffe and with a commanding view of Mt. Kilimanjaro 110 miles away. "It was just thrilling seeing from the doorstep the tallest animals in the world standing in front of the tallest mountain in Africa," owner Betty Leslie-Melville said of her first impression of the house.

The massive marble entrance opens onto 120 acres of park land (opposite page, upper left). It leads into a formal entrance hall where a portrait of Betty Leslie-Melville hangs over the fireplace (right). The office (above) is headquarters to the African Fund for Endangered Wildlife founded by the Leslie-Melvilles. A mahogany staircase leads to the stately bedrooms, some containing Karen Blixen's original furniture (opposite page, right).

He met his wife, Betty, an American from Baltimore, at the Kenyan seaside resort of Malindi.

Together, in Nairobi, Betty and Jock raised Betty's children, Rick, McDonnel, and Dancy, and two adopted babies, Daisy and Marlon, who inspired the Leslie-Melvilles to found the African Fund for Endangered Wildlife (AFEW). "A friend told us that he had the only 130 Rothschild giraffes in the world on his ranch and that they were being poached," Betty said "We told him we'd adopt one, Daisy, and later adopted another, Marlon."

The only people to raise wild giraffe successfully, the Leslie-Melvilles translocated four breeding groups of Rothschild giraffe to parks formerly free of other giraffe. As a result of AFEW, there are now nearly 500 in Kenya and growing.

"When we brought Daisy home, her head protruding from the minivan sunroof, an African told us it was the first time he had ever seen a giraffe," Betty remembered. "Because many Africans can't afford park fees, we set up a wildlife center here where African children are bused in for educational programs."

American children, too, benefited from Betty's achievements: Former first lady Barbara Bush personally chose Betty's book, *Daisy Rothschild*, to read on the radio for her literacy program. Like H. Rider Haggard before her, Betty was invited to the White House to share her African adventures with the president, his wife, and the American public.

"*In the highlands, you woke in the morning and thought: Here I am, where I ought to be.*"

—Karen Blixen, *Out of Africa*

The hosts at Giraffe Manor really stick their neck out to make sure guests enjoy "family-style" dining—a term that takes on a new meaning at the home of seven giraffe, 40 warthog, and several retired polo ponies.

To wander through the house is like journeying through Kenyan history. Books and press clippings document the family's involvement in Kenyan politics and conservation.

hospitality kudos

Like the migrant herds, settler hospitality doesn't stop at national boundaries. The Rattray Reserves —one of the largest private game reserves in the world—comprising Kirkman's Homestead (left) and MalaMala , won highest accolades from **Condé Nast** *for being the top resort in the world.*

South African hunter homestead Kirkman's and the associated resort, MalaMala, are both part of the Rattray Reserves, located in the Sabi Sands Game Reserve, a cooperative of exclusive properties adjacent to the Kruger National Park.

By 1869, when the name MalaMala was first associated with the property, ranching and hunting had already decimated the game in this area. Although it was declared a protected area by the first president of the Transvaal, Paul Kruger, it was not until the Rattray family, the current owners, introduced careful game management and conservation practices that the wild game flourished once again.

With the end of apartheid, foreigners are packing their bags for the Sabi Sands for one compelling reason: At MalaMala and Kirkman's, visitors are virtually guaranteed to bag the Big Five within days of arrival.

Shooting, however, is strictly photographic—today, clients want a mounted photo, not a mounted head. However, having a ranger who can cock a camera as fast as a rifle is all part of the MalaMala mystique.

Dashing young men with polished accents, the guides resembled a

Manicured lawns, shady verandas, and bougainvillea-covered villas give the impression of a make-believe "DisneyVeld." But the combination of solicitous hospitality with unpredictable adventure delivers a once-in-a-lifetime experience at both MalaMala (above) and Kirkman's Homestead (left).

The Dutch arrived here in
1725 seeking the empire of
Monomatapa, the source of the
Queen of Sheba's riches. Instead,
they found one of Africa's greatest
treasures: a game habitat that is
home to the Big Five. The mounted
game trophies in the bar at
MalaMala date back to its early
days as a hunting ground.

Here, a century later, Cornwallis
Harris was the first European to
observe "a magnificent coal–black
buck…with scimitar–shaped
horns," more impressive "than all
the elephants of Africa." The
Sable antelope, or malamala in
Shangaan, became the namesake
of the former hunting lodge,
where, now, shooting is only done
with cameras.

cast call for potential sitcoms like *Bush-watch* or *Ranger-Rogues*. Settling into an open Land Rover, we were coddled with soft woolen blankets thrown over our bare legs. "Hello, my name's Jamie and I'll be your ranger," our guide greeted with all the obsequiousness of a Beverly Hills headwaiter—except for the rifle over his shoulder. "Don't stand up. Don't yell out. Don't walk off," he commanded as we set off for a game drive.

It seemed simple...until a black mamba slithered across the road. I rose off my seat for a better look. Even at 20 feet, the deadly snake instantly reared two feet off the ground, its head swinging like a compass needle searching for its bearing: me! Fortunately, it whipped off into the grass, stunning me with nothing worse than surprise.

Hanging above the mantel of his old homestead is a portrait of Harry Kirkman, one of the first game wardens at Kruger National Park. The entrance to the farmhouse pub displays old Dutch china and glass (right).

"NOWHERE IS THAT MYSTERIOUS PRESENCE OF WILD AFRICA FELT MORE DEEPLY THAN IN THE TRANSVAAL LOWVELD," WROTE FIELD MARSHAL JAN SMUTS IN 1929 AFTER VISITING THE LOCATION OF MALAMALA AND KIRKMAN'S.

The dining room at MalaMala is situated on a game-viewing platform that hangs over a lush meadow, often frequented by warthogs, impala, elephants, and an occasional leopard.

Sunset was approaching and our sights were on sundowners. While Jamie unloaded a hamper with hors d'oeuvres and champagne, one of my companions wandered down to a waterhole—where she encountered a leopard.

Soundlessly, Jamie materialized with the gun. Instantly we were in the Jeep, slipping into gear. Lolling in the grass was a young leopard—luckily, without its protective mother. I suddenly understood why today's guides still need the charms of a gentleman but all the valor of a professional hunter.

Hospitality in the settler days consisted of a warm welcome, a shared meal, and good conversation. Successive generations of settler families have expanded these expectations to include gourmet meals, esoteric culture, and adrenaline-pumping adventures. But it remains the unique personality of the settler—independent, innovative, and convivial—that delivers what travelers have always sought to bring home from safari: tales to tell, head shots to mount, and friends to keep.

"To wander through a fairyland among a new and fabled creation is truly spirit-stirring and romantic."

—Sir William Cornwallis Harris

Tent
En Suite

*The classic Manyara tent, popular
since Roosevelt's time, remains the
mainstay at today's tented camps—
but with a new twist at luxury camps
like Galdessa (opposite page),
Savanna (upper left), and Abu's
(above).*

Many travelers today yearn for the adventure of safari combined with the security of home. They want to see the bush, not get bushed. They want wild creatures, but with all the creature comforts. They lust for the romance of safari, but think romance begins with a bubble bath. Like the settlers, they don't want to give up what they've enjoyed in the past just to acquire a new experience.

Today's safari operators adhere to the same rule: Like mixing a good sundowner, they've extracted the essence of the quintessential fly-camps, sweetened it with old-fashioned settler hospitality, and spiked it with modern conveniences. Tent deck floors paved the way. En suite bathrooms removed the biggest drawback to the bush. Thus, "tent en suite" was erected.

Long-drop toilets are long gone, but canvas, camaraderie, and civility remain. Canvas is the common denominator of both old and new camps. For in the deep African night, strange and wonderful noises that are heard in a tent could be muted by walls. Each sound becomes an intense personal encounter on the wild side: the snap of a twig (an impala?), a punctuated hiss (a serval cat??) the crash of a fallen branch (an elephant??!).

Then, suddenly, the undeniable sound of a lion's roar: beginning as a few moans, crescendoing to a series of thunderous roars, and concluding with a string of grunts. According to the East Africans, the lion is claiming in Swahili, *"Nchi ya nani? Yangu, yangu, YANGU!"* ("Whose land is this? Mine, mine, MINE!")

At the tent en suite, guests are filled with awe for the elemental magic of Africa. The look, the smell, the feel of the bush permeates the tent and seeps into the soul. As travel writer John Heminway recalled, even before departing, you "find yourself missing it with an almost physical longing."

the safari game

"I WAS WILD TO KNOW WHAT AFRICA WAS LIKE? WHAT DO THEY DO? THE COUNTRY— THE ANIMALS?"

—KATHARINE HEPBURN, *THE MAKING OF THE AFRICAN QUEEN*

In the stampede to bag the Big Five, travelers overlook the equal beauty of smaller mammals and birds. Sometimes the best way to turn on to Africa is to turn off the engine. Relaxing at camp or sitting in a hide proves that often "less is more."

At Swala Camp, forgoing a game drive in order to photograph the camp, I stepped out of the tent for a wider angle. In my peripheral vision, a dark blur disturbed the monotony of the golden savanna. Turning, I saw a lean, black-maned lion stalk past the tent, through camp, and off to a nearby watering hole, where he drank lazily before disappearing again into the bush.

Another day, at Sekanani, we set off at dawn with a picnic hamper in the direction of lion roars we'd heard the night before. Guided by vultures, we found the lions devouring a kill and watched as nature's pecking order of lion, lioness, cub, jackal, hyena, and vulture took their turn at a breakfast of fresh zebra.

Later, we spread a picnic blanket in the middle of a zebra herd. Seated at ground level, we suddenly understood the unlikely camouflage effect created from contrasting stripes viewed through blades of grass, which produces a disturbing moiré pattern, foiling predators' attempts to distinguish weak or young individuals from the herd.

In the afternoon, we found a cheetah mother nursing her three fluffy cubs under the shade of a thorn tree. Stretched out in the Jeep, close enough to hear the soft chirps of the cubs, we took turns napping as the cats slept. Our patience was rewarded when the mother stretched and spied an impala. Stealthily, she led the cubs off in its direction, while we

An orphaned cheetah, Queenie (bottom), had to be taught by rangers how to hunt. Reintroduced into the wild, she now teaches her cubs how to hunt—and teaches overzealous filmmakers the need to respect distance from the game (opposite page).

Tented camps in the Maasai Mara, the Serengeti, and Tarangire such as Sekanani (opposite page) combine all the comforts of home with something few homes boast—a view into the family life of the wild creatures of the African plains, like this cheetah family of the Mara.

followed at an appropriate distance. But, as happens, another Jeep cut ahead of the predators for a better view. Alerted, the impala bounded and the cubs scattered, but the mother cheetah, unfazed, sprang onto the top of the vehicle, providing a great shot for all except the passengers of the inconsiderate Jeep.

Alternating between long spells of wildlife observation and long rides through the open plains, we gained a sense of integration with the African wildlife. Whereas the lodges in the Sabi Sands deliver the volume and proximity of animals portrayed by Imax films, small tented camps in East Africa offer the freedom and tranquillity reflected in Karen Blixen's prose.

"It was only my second night in Africa, yet something had begun to grow inside me, as if my childhood dreams had finally found the place where they could materialize. I had arrived where I was always meant to be. I was certain without any shadow of doubt that it was here that I wanted to live. I was in love with Africa."

—Kuki Gallmann, *I Dreamed of Africa*

Machado Luxury Tented Safari's Swala Camp (below) in Tanzania's Tarangire National Park is decorated with the bright colors of the East African coast.

Overnight camping on deserted sandbar islands (left) and deep-sea fishing safaris are offered to Machado's guests at a plantation resort on the shores of the Indian Ocean.

Governor's Camps
Maasai Mara
Kenya

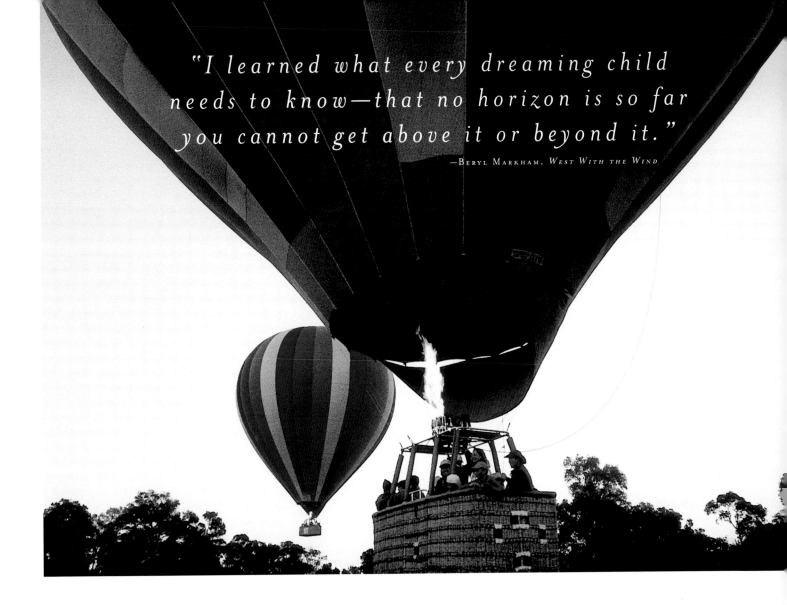

"I learned what every dreaming child needs to know—that no horizon is so far you cannot get above it or beyond it."

—BERYL MARKHAM, *WEST WITH THE WIND*

safari on the fly

Built at the site where Teddy Roosevelt camped in the Maasai Mara, Governor's Camps carries a cachet in the safari social set, who flock in droves for the unique experience of a "safari on the fly."

Gathering in an open field in the predawn darkness, guests sip warm drinks while brightly colored hot-air balloons are inflated. As the sun pushes up over the horizon, the balloons fill and lift off the ground.

Twelve awestruck passengers gingerly step into the wicker basket of each balloon. Like a stream of champagne bubbles rising in a golden orb, the balloons float up into the dawn sky. Spirits lift, too: *Now, this is living with all cylinders firing!* I thought.

In the heart of the best game–
viewing area of the Maasai Mara,
the setting for the Governor's
Family of Camps is so sublime
that at the turn of the century
it was reserved exclusively for
Kenya's colonial governors and
their royal visitors. Four exclusive
campsites hug the winding
banks of the Mara River,
a favorite haunt for hippo,
elephant, and leopard.

I recalled aviatrix Beryl Markham's comment when, piloted by Denys Finch Hatton, she took her first flight above Africa, many years before her world-record flight from Nairobi to London: "When you fly, you get a feeling of possession that you couldn't have if you owned all of Africa." Karen Blixen, too, said that flying over the African plains was "the most transporting pleasure of my life."

Unperturbed by the round shadow creeping across the plains, the normally skittish herds of plains animals interact tranquilly. Like a god in the sky, you feel you could reach down and touch the toy menagerie below.

But the safari ritual of a hearty breakfast can't be burst even by a hot-air balloon excursion. "Heads down!" yelled the pilot as we slowly bumped to a landing on the open grassland, where the balloons unloaded their passengers for a banquet of mixed grill, barbecued over the flames of the cylinders. Champagne corks fly through the air—a Governor's salute to another new day in Africa.

"Once you fly, you will walk with your eyes skyward, for there you have been, and there you will go again."

an african romance

"Visitors to Africa want an *Out of Africa* experience," said Peter Frank, whose camp is dedicated to the memory of Africa's most famous love affair, between Denys Finch Hatton and Karen Blixen.

"Denys Finch Hatton personifies the romance of safari," Peter explained. "The seduction of his personality is as powerful today as it was in his lifetime."

The second son of the Earl of Winchelsea, Finch Hatton came to Africa at 23 years old and quickly became the most eligible hunter. A favorite safari companion was Karen Blixen, the wife of his best friend, Baron Bror Blixen ("Blix"). Unperturbed, Blix introduced Finch Hatton as "*my* best friend and *my wife's* lover"—after all, everyone on Blix's safaris knew that clients accompanied by their wives were wise to bring an unattached female for the Baron.[1]

A frequent visitor at the Blixens', Finch Hatton kept the household stocked with books, music, and cigars. He also kept a room in Nairobi at the Muthaiga Club, where he or the Baron stayed between safari engagements.

Together they took on safari the Prince of Wales, the future Edward VIII of England—while another of

Denys Finch Hatton's insistence
on meticulously planned safaris
and elegant surroundings is
reflected at the Tsavo camp
named in his honor. The formal
teak bedroom and Victorian-style
bathroom contrast with a Lamu
bed covered in the colorful
"katanga" worn by the Swahili
women of Kenya's coast.

Overhanging the hippo-churned
lagoon, a private veranda at each
tent provides unlimited wildlife
viewing that would have made this
the type of setting Finch Hatton
might have chosen for his home.

their entourage, Beryl Markham, entertained the prince's brother back in London, scampering barefoot through Buckingham Palace and hiding from Queen Mary in a bedroom cupboard.

The romantic focus of many women, Denys taught Karen how to hunt lion by foot and taught Beryl how to track game by air. Only the sixth sense of Beryl's mentor, who convinced her to cancel a flight with Finch Hatton, prevented Beryl from joining him on his last flight. Another friend, Margaret Layell, was also forced to turn down Finch Hatton's invitation for "a quick dip before I leave" by her young daughter's hysterical screams that the plane would crash. Within minutes of takeoff, the Gypsy Moth's engine stuttered and the plane plummeted to the ground.

All his life, Finch Hatton resisted settling down, but Peter Frank has cre-

ated the type of home he might have had. Everything is done in style. Guests are encouraged to dress formally for dinner just as the settlers and White Hunters did on their evenings "on the town" at the Muthaiga. Regal seven-course repasts are based on recipes that Finch Hatton used on safari, while strains of classical music float through the African night, recalling Denys' gift of a gramophone to Karen. An African love affair still carries on at Finch Hatton's.

Outside, a rowdy crowd belches with rude insensitivity to the refined atmosphere—a pod of resident hippo plod along the muddy banks toward the lagoon. Even more than the camp's proclivity for the good life, its proximity to the wildlife would have made Denys Finch Hatton feel at home at the camp that bears his name.

Exposed timber beams, shining dark wooden floors, and antique
kilim rugs in the dining room (opposite page, top), smoking room
(opposite page, bottom), and library (above) are reminiscent of the
Blixens' farm, where Denys Finch Hatton sought companionship.

a tent with a view

An alternative to the action-packed routines of other camps made sense to camp owner Pierre Mourgue d'Algue and manager Stephanie Kuna, who parachuted from the fast-paced world of stock brokerage into the safari world. A French-Swiss stockbroker based in London and New York, Pierre first got involved in the camp as a silent partner. At the time, his attention was focused on London-based Latinvest Securities, a merchant bank specializing in Latin America, which he cofounded in 1992.

"Initially, my interest in Galdessa was as a financial partner," he explained. "I was a banker in love with the bush who wanted a little pad in the wilderness for my free time." After five years, when Latinvest rated as the second best merchant bank in the United Kingdom and Europe, Pierre sold his shares in Latinvest, bought out his partner in Galdessa, and completely rebuilt the camp.

Stephanie was also a top-ranking stockbroker, one of the first women to work at the Chicago office of Horn-blower and Weeks. In her latest incarnation of a peripatetic career, she has been instrumental in defining the look and taste of Galdessa, one of Africa's most ecology-conscious camps.

"*In wilderness is the preservation of the world.*"
—HENRY DAVID THOREAU

"Our objective has been to build structures in harmony with the setting," Galdessa owner Pierre Mourgue d'Algue (below) states. Instead of clearing trees, the trunks of five majestic palms were incorporated into the architecture of the Main River Lodge (opposite page) and the Honeymoon Suite (right).

Galdessa's unique architecture is a fusion of safari tent and boma (a traditional thatched hut): The walls are constructed of both adobe and canvas; doors and windows zip open, but the ceiling is a lofty thatched roof. Sun-bleached driftwood is sculpted into beds, and slabs of local Galena paving stones are fashioned into graceful tables.

The emphasis at Galdessa is not on the Big Five treasure hunt; rather, it is on the integration of nature and the soul. "It's easy to see the elephant that pass through camp—especially at the plunge pool of the honeymoon suite!" Stephanie explained. "But their only living relative, the little rock hyrax, is just as interesting to observe."

"'The real voyage of discovery consists not in seeking new landscape, but in seeing with new eyes,'" Pierre said, quoting Proust. "I'm a wildlife lover who got lost in the world of finance. I've come back to conservation to apply my perspective and experience gained in investment banking because, ultimately, the need for the wilderness to become an economic resource, with greater value preserved than destroyed, becomes its only chance for survival."

The catch of the day, fresh fish from the Galena River, is one of the delicacies served by Galdessa's chef, renowned for healthy "safari spa" menus.

Rather than importing accessories, Galdessa has developed a local cottage craft industry. Wall sconces are made from ostrich eggs and buffalo vertebrae. Safari chairs in leather and canvas combine to create a new look.

"NATURE IS THE MOST IMPORTANT THING IN OUR LIVES AND THE CLOSER PEOPLE AND ANIMALS ARE RELATED, THE MORE...LIFE-ENHANCING IT WILL BE."
—PETER BEARD, *THE ADVENTURES AND MISADVENTURES OF PETER BEARD*

An oasis in the vast Zambezi National Park, the cascading water of the multitiered pool at Matetsi Safari Camp is a contemporary interpretation of nearby Victoria Falls.

The camp's decorating theme of colonial nostalgia is inspired by the falls' Victorian railroad station built in 1905, a relic of Cecil Rhodes' dream of a Cape Town–to–Cairo rail line.

staying on track

Safari travelers today can take satisfaction in the fact that, by virtue of their trip, they are effectively contributing to wildlife conservation. "Here at Matetsi Safari Camp, we employ 40 Zimbabweans," explained camp manager Peter Dunning. "In Africa, on average, each working person supports about 10 other people, so, in reality, the camp is supporting about 400 local Africans."

Matetsi Safari Camp is one of more than 20 exclusive camps run by Conservation Corporation of Africa (Conscorp). With an international board of shareholders such as members of the Getty family, Hambros P.L.C., Sakura Bank of Japan, and Southern Sun Hotels of South Africa, its mission is to prove that capitalism and ecotourism can be effective tools in grassroots economic development and regional wildlife conservation.

At Conscorp properties, local Africans are hired at all levels, from busboys to camp managers. To help local communities keep on track, Conscorp builds schools, libraries, clinics, and laboratories. Its Rural Investment Fund acts as a catalyst for the integrated growth of local development projects for the camps.

An example of Conscorp's philosophy is the case of poacher Zibane Mazibuka. Too poor to pay the fine levied by the local tribe, he was assigned three months' unpaid work making bricks by hand for Conscorp.

Conscorp then helped him buy brickmaking machinery, and he now employs 10 workers making bricks for local clients, including Conscorp.

Conscorp realizes, as do other camps, that the larger the stake local people have in eco-tourism, the less likely they will be to poach wildlife. As the letter greeting every guest explains, "You represent a vital link in the chain of evidence that wildlife tourism is the most viable economic option in many remote parts of Africa. Your visit helps to ensure that this continent's wild places remain in perpetuity for future generations."

In the tents, the bedroom furniture is built from old "sleepers," the phrase used by the colonists for railway ties. The classic safari experience sought by the train passengers arriving from

Cape Town is achieved through the use of tented ceilings, cream walls hung with African art, animal-print fabric, thick timber centerposts, old-fashioned bathtubs, overhead fans, and wall-to-wall sisal matting.

trunks up!

While Conscorp funds schools for African children, Abu Camp also runs a school—for elephants! The Elephant Training School is the pet project of Randall Moore, an American zoologist from Portland, Oregon. On the first true African game safari, Cornwallis Harris had fantasized about riding African elephants through the plains as he had done on their Asian relatives in India. Randall has made the dream a reality for guests who explore the Okavango on the backs of Abu and his family.

"My career as a perennial zoology student took an abrupt detour when I inherited three fully grown elephants from the widow of my first employer, exotic animal trainer Morgan Berry," Randall explained. "With no home of my own to accommodate them, I resolved to return them to their own home—Africa!"

He convinced the American Broadcasting Company to sponsor the four-year odyssey, which became the subject of his book, *Back to Africa,* and two award-winning documentaries. After returning the elephants to their homeland, he started returning elephants to the workplace—in the film business.

An avid cigar aficionado and exotic animal trainer, Oregon native Randall Moore designed a camp that combines the masculinity of a private smoking club with the glamour of show business.

Camp headquarters is a magnificent green canvas structure with a graceful arched profile, evocative of the Sydney Opera House, surrounded by century-old fig trees. (Left) Randall's prodigy, Abu, starred with Clint Eastwood in **White Hunter, Black Heart**. Between film appearances, Abu and his family take privileged safari travelers on elephant-back through the pristine wilderness of the Okavango Delta.

Trunk touching tongue, Baby
Seba gives Kathy an elephant kiss.
Observation decks encircling guest
tents (left) and the main tent
(opposite page, top and bottom)
provide intimate views of animal
behavior.

Acquiring a trio of trained African elephants in the States, he led them to their screen premiere in *Circles in a Forest*. Since then the same trio—Abu, Kathy, and Bennie—has starred in such international films as *White Hunter, Black Heart*; *Lost in Africa*; *The Power of One*; *Sirga*; and *Master of Elephants*.

The trio has now grown to a family of six adults, a boisterous Brat Pack of seven juveniles, and baby Seba. Although Abu, Kathy, and Bennie continue to journey worldwide on assignment, they now attract people from all over the world to their own unique location, Abu Camp.

Stepping onto Abu's bent knee, I climbed aboard to view the Okavango from an elephant's perspective. "The elephant scent masks the human one, so a wide variety of game from cheetah and lion to wild dog and waterbuck are not alarmed and allow visitors to get incredibly close," Randall explained. The elephants can track lions on the hunt, even following them as they swim between the islands, while riders stay dry on top of the elephants' mighty backs.

As the caravan silently ambled along, I absorbed the sounds, signs, and smells of the wilderness. The mahoots led us along fresh pug tracks until we spied a lioness and cub resting in the grass. Respectful of their space, Randall silently motioned for the mahoots to lead the herd to a waterhole for a playful mud-bath, while we remained securely strapped in the saddle.

In the evening, the campfire, cigars, and port bonded guests and guides. Aware that Randall Moore had provided us with a once-in-a-lifetime experience that, like the legendary memory of elephants, we would never forget, we raised our glasses to him and his family of elephants, with a hearty toast: "Trunks up!"

Five luxuriously appointed guest tents (above and opposite page, top) and a spacious main tent (right and opposite page, bottom) sport animal-skin prints and antique ethnic furniture.

"IT IS A RARE PHENOMENON IN OUR TIMES FOR A MAN
TO DO SOMETHING NEVER BEFORE DONE. RANDALL
MOORE HAS DONE PRECISELY THAT," WROTE
DR. ANTHONY HALL-MARTIN, CHIEF RESEARCH
OFFICER OF THE NATIONAL PARKS OF SOUTH AFRICA
ABOUT RANDALL'S REHABILITATION OF AFRICAN
ELEPHANTS. "THE SIGNIFICANCE OF HIS WORK
BECOMES MORE APPARENT BY THE DAY...FOR THE
OPTIONS IT HOLDS FOR THE FUTURE."

"Tonight our campsite echoes to the squeal of baboons, the rumblings of nearby hippos feeding and an elephant felling a fruit-filled palm tree. We sleep like children."

—HORST KLEMM, *AN AFRICAN JOURNAL*

Game-viewing verandas on raised platforms overlook the watery wilderness of the Okavango Delta. Not only do tents offer complete privacy and access to nature, they also have solar-powered electricity, hot water, and old-fashioned porcelain bathtubs with elegant brass fixtures.

Offering ultimate luxury in a setting often called Africa's "Last Eden," Abu Camp has become a favorite retreat for well-heeled safari travelers and a sought-after location for fashion shoots and film productions.

springtime in savanna

Inevitably, "Africa" conjures up yellow hues. "I speak of Africa, of golden days," says Shakespeare's King Henry VII (along with Teddy Roosevelt and Ernest Hemingway). The golden grasslands of the Serengeti, tawny lions' manes, amber leopard spots, creamy impala, saffron sunsets, and dusty khaki shorts: These are the colors of Africa in the dry season, the traditional safari season.

Parched by drought, a landscape of bare trees and burned grass makes it simple to spot game. But to each season there is a time, and for the sheer exuberance and variety of game, there's no season like spring.

Arriving at Savanna at the beginning of December, I found Africa transformed. The rain had washed the golden grasslands green. Everywhere new life was bursting with animation

Duncan and Louise Rodgers are camp hosts at Savanna Tented Camp, a refreshing new camp in the Sabi Sands Private Game Reserve in South Africa.

like a Disney fairy-tale classic: butterflies flitted from meadow blooms, birds swooped from half-built nests, and tree branches were swollen with buds.

Also swollen with offspring were the zebra mares, impala does, and wildebeest females. Everywhere little African Bambis crouched hidden in thickets of lush grass, revealed only by an occasional wide-eyed peep at the big metal beast lumbering past them.

"The mass birthing of these herds is timed with the arrival of the fresh sprouts of grass," explained our guide Duncan, who lives with his own baby daughter and wife at the camp. "The sheer volume of all these newborns at one time ensures that sufficient numbers will survive to maintain the breeding herd even after the predators have had their pick."

Well fattened on the plentiful supply of succulent delicacies, the lions, leopards, and cheetahs were at their prime, sporting glossy velvet

Spring provides the design theme at Savanna. Mint-green tent tarps cap the main lodge and guest cottages (previous page). Inside, white canvas tented ceilings undulate with the breeze. Flowers and insect motifs adorn the room. A short hop from Johannesburg, this is an ideal camp to start a safari on a romantic note or to end a safari on a natural high.

coats. While I was there both lions and leopards were mating repeatedly with all the recklessness of teenagers on spring break.

With the rains return flocks of migratory birds. A frenzy of nest building is much in evidence: Bright yellow weavers weave oval nests that hang like tidy bird condos from the marula trees. Even the insects are engaging: Amethyst scarabs busily roll a food ball as large as a golf ball across the road, the male pushing it with his back legs while his mate rides, frantically jiggling like a circus performer to maintain her position on top of the rolling ball.

Nighttime, too, has a different tone. The fiery bronze sunsets of dust-laden summer skies give way to soft tones of lavender-rose. The air is clear—day's backdrop of billowing white clouds against a sparkling blue sky transforms to night's deep claret bowl studded with iridescent stars. The cuckoo sings a song of courtship well into the night, accompanied by a deafening chorus of rattling, bubbling, croaking, and trilling frogs.

Against this background of fecundity and profusion, Savanna reflects a mood as fresh and airy as cotton sheets line-dried on a bright, breezy day. "We wanted a change from the traditional safari style, so we mixed florals with animal prints," Duncan's wife, Louise, explained. "We even found some wonderful insect motifs!" The overall effect is a refreshingly different, but entirely apropos, approach to "safari romantic."

"I love not Man the less, but Nature more."

—Lord Byron

> *"Entering a wildlife sanctuary is a rare, gratifying, and sometimes humbling experience. We hope Africa is that for you..."*
>
> —Dave Varty

Following Thoreau's philosophy, guests are encouraged to commune with nature.

Like Hemingway's heroes, clients develop character as fear is replaced by an understanding of the animals.

Just as the Tent En Suite offers a modern adaptation of the lifestyle of the professional hunters, there is a contemporary version of the settler homesteads—Nature En Suite.

At the quintessential fly-camps and the Tent En Suite camps, the focus was on game; adventure and adrenaline charged the atmosphere. At the Nature En Suite camps, the emphasis is on the setting; simplicity and serenity soothe the soul.

These camps are not made of canvas, but of boulders and boughs, rocks and reeds. They are designed to expose guests to the nurturing side of nature, rather than protecting them from its dangers.

But, as the Tent En Suite indulges a basic hunter instinct, the Nature En Suite camps satisfy a primitive need of humans to seek shelter where they feel comfortably protected, yet have an outlook onto the environment. British geographer Jay Appleton calls it the "prospect-refuge" syndrome, theorizing that it might be triggered by a genetic memory of living on the forest edge (refuge) and scanning the open plains (prospect) for enemies or prey.

At the treehouses, river retreats, and stone sanctuaries throughout Africa, this emotion has been given rein. Freer in spirit and bolder in shape than conventional dwellings, these camps are a contemporary manifestation of the innovative character of the settler personality.

Here, style has more to do with vision and view than action and accomplishment. Presenting a unique vantage point from which to experience the sheer power and majesty of the African landscape, the Nature En Suite camp completes the safari experience.

Nature
En Suite

"*Even the greatest bird must come down from the sky to find a tree to roost on.*"

—BUSHMAN PROVERB

safari love nest

The treehouses of Ngong House on the outskirts of Nairobi represent the free-flying spirit of owner Paul Verleysen. Arriving in Africa in 1970, Paul worked as a teacher of architecture in the Congo and Rwanda before accepting a diplomatic posting at the Belgian embassy in Nairobi. When Paul heard his next assignment would take him to another continent, he decided to leave the diplomatic service rather than leave Africa.

He bought an old hunter homestead in Langata on the outskirts of Nairobi, where he designed the type of house he had dreamed of when he

first taught architecture—a treehouse. Typical of the Nature En Suite camps, the intrinsic appeal of Paul's treehouses is the fact that they have been built from the heart and capture the spirit of freedom.

"Even though we are on the outskirts of the capital, I wanted to build an environment integrated with nature," Paul explained. "By putting guests at treetop level, I hope that they will tune in to the incredible avi-fauna that this country offers." The size of

Handcrafted log cabins on stilts constructed from round tree trunks instead of split timber are approached via a spiral staircase of polished wood.

The first floor accommodates the living room, kitchenette, bathroom, and deck. Loft bedrooms are tucked under the eaves of the thatched roof.

Each treehouse derives its decorating theme from one of the four compass points. The North Treehouse is decorated in icy blues and greens with cool wrought-iron furniture (opposite page). The East Treehouse luxuriates with rich Oriental reds and exotic treasures from the Far East (this page).

Texas, Kenya has more than 1,000 different bird species, while in all of North America there are only 703. As a result, it's easy to spot 100 different species a day.

Each treehouse is different but equally stunning—sensual and cozy as a lovebird's nest. This same refined atmosphere is mirrored at the dinner table. A Belgian chef prepares food so beautifully that each meal becomes an epicurean indulgence on par with the best restaurants in Europe. Unlike traditional treehouses, the luxurious hideaways at Ngong House are definitely not for the birds!

Local crafts incorporate nature into the decor: frames made from porcupine quills and Maasai knives (above), stained-glass windows (below), and naturally dyed wool throws (right).

a wild touch

Touch of the Wild's treehouses are treetop hides towering over watering holes in Hwange, one of Africa's great conservation achievements, where Touch of the Wild founder Alan Elliot contributed to its success.

Located on the tip of the Kalahari Desert, Hwange is devoid of any perennial surface water and is incapable of naturally sustaining much life—animal or human. In the 1920s, local settlers created a game park by boring for water to create 60 artificial waterholes.

The success of Hwange is reflected in the history of the resident Presidential Elephants. In 1972, a herd of 20 delinquent elephants, traumatized by poachers, was moved to a private game reserve where they were rehabilitated, multiplying to a herd of 300.

In 1991, Alan Elliot convinced President Robert Mugabe of Zimbabwe to grant the herd official protection. Now the herd wanders freely, and Hwange boasts one of the densest elephant populations in Africa.

Touch of the Wild
operates four safari
camps in Hwange.
Guests are accommodated
in rustic treehouses
with en suite bathrooms.

Like the Mara, Serengeti, and Sabi Sands, Hwange teams with wildlife—but not with tourists. The land is more arid than the other ecosystems, but, as a result, animals predictably congregate at the artificial watering holes. To protect the fragile vegetation that controls the spread of the desert, off-road cross-country drives are prohibited. Instead, strategically positioned observation platforms command stunning views over the well-frequented watering holes.

These wonderful lookouts can be reserved for overnight camp-outs. On a budget camping trip with my two young children, we alternated nights in our backpacker's tent pitched at Hwange Main Camp with nights in sleeping bags on top of the observation decks. The discomfort of lying awake on a hard floor, the fear that hyena would break the barricade to eat our shoes, and the absence of a campfire was more than offset by the thrill of watching, under the full moon, a large matriarchal herd of elephants materialize, like a midnight mirage. Single file, they paraded to the edge of the watering hole, where they drank,

bathed, and dusted themselves before silently gliding away like silvery ghosts.

At Touch of the Wild, travelers experience mystical moonlit game viewing—with the comfort of a soft mattress, an en suite bathroom, and a lockable door. While Hwange's plat-

forms let travelers observe unobtrusively the complex social relationships of animals, Touch of the Wild treehouses extend this privilege even further—allowing you to stay up at night with the animals, but to fall asleep in your own treetop bed.

LOCAL FABRICS, POTTERY, AND
CRAFTS ACCESSORIZE THE INTERIORS
OF TOUCH OF THE WILD'S TREEHOUSE
CAMPS (LOWER RIGHT) AND THE
KATCHANA LODGE (LEFT).

the leopard's lair

Hwange's Touch of the Wild tree-houses are designed for living above the animals, but Londolozi Tree Camp gained success from its owners' reputation of living *amidst* the animals. The Varty brothers—David, John, and Shan—are to leopards what the Adamsons, *Born Free* author Joy and her husband, George, were to lions. Their ability to raise and rehabilitate leopards led to the creation of Londolozi and, ultimately, to Conscorp.

The same company that runs Matetsi, Conscorp's story dates back to 1926. At a tennis party, Charles Boyd Varty heard about a game farm, Sparta, for sale. Enthused by President Kruger's recent proclamation of Kruger

Guest treehouses are hidden among enormous jackalberry trees (above). A catwalk leads to a secluded niche in the forest canopy. Surrounded by a wide wooden veranda and shaded with matchstick blinds, the muted tones of the treetop loft recall the dappled coat of the resident leopards.

"During my long walk to freedom, I had the rare privilege to visit Londolozi. There I saw people of all races living in harmony amidst the beauty that Mother Nature offers."

—Nelson Mandela

National Park in the same area, he bought Sparta on the spot, sight unseen.

Charles and, later, his son, Boyd, used Sparta as a private hunting ground. But when Boyd died in 1969, his sons, only in their early twenties, transformed it into a wildlife reserve. They called it Londolozi, Zulu for "protector of all living things."

In particular, Londolozi came to signify a haven for leopards. The Vartys had a talent for rearing abandoned leopard cubs and rehabilitating them into the wild. Acclimated to humans, the leopards of Londolozi became a unique attraction of the Sabi Sands Game Reserve.

Given their penchant for leopards, it seemed appropriate to build their lodge among the branches of the riverine forest that hugs the banks of the Sand River. Balanced on tall stilts, the main lodge juts out from the rock boulders over the river, giving spectacular open views of the leopards' favorite habitat.

The first safari lodge to be awarded the coveted Relais & Chateaux rating, Londolozi's success led to the creation of Conscorp. The accomplishment of the Varty boys was acknowledged by Nelson Mandela, president of South Africa, who said, "Londolozi represents a model of the dream I cherish for the future of nature preservation in our country."

The modern style of Londolozi Main Camp is as indigenous as the ethnic look of Londolozi Tree Camp. As Warren Robbins, founding director emeritus at the National Museum of African Art in Washington, D.C., points out, "Modern art would not be what it is today if the European artist had not come into contact with African art and borrowed many of its images and concepts."

Inspired by nature, like the stripes of a zebra's flank, and by ethnic art, like the traditional mud cloth, Londolozi decorators create innovative accents—including door handles cast from antelope horns and ostrich eggs etched with black pigment.

A palette of aqua, wine, moss, and sand complements the riverine environment. A flowing net of muslin encases the master bedroom in a seductive mood.

EACH CHALET IS INCORPORATED
INTO THE SURROUNDING GRANITE
ROCK—LIKE THE OUTDOOR SHOWER
AND DECK—UNIFYING THE
STRUCTURE WITH THE NATURAL
WORLD AROUND IT.

The avant-garde modern style asserts a progressive South African confidence in the future. The contrast in sensibilities between classic safari and contemporary Africa is reflected in the materials used: Stone, thatch, and wood are symbols of the old; concrete, steel, and tile represent the new.

A SPACIOUS BATHROOM BECOMES A "SAFARI SPA" WITH REED AND DARK, CHISELED WOOD
DOORS (ABOVE) LEADING OUT TO A PRIVATE PLUNGE POOL. IN THE MAIN LODGE, A COLLECTION OF
COOKING SPOONS AND UTENSILS IS DISPLAYED IN FRONT OF THE FIREPLACE (RIGHT).

river retreats

Although treehouses were well suited for the first Londolozi Camp, when Conscorp started building additional lodges, the company recruited local designers to translate traditional safari concepts into a modern South African idiom. Each camp has a unique identity inspired by the environment and executed in Conscorp's signature style.

At Matetsi Water Lodge, the sister camp of Matetsi Safari Camp, the architects envisioned a luxurious river hideaway. Located on Zimbabwe's Zambezi River, the architecture borrows elements from the local heritage. As evidenced by many Stone Age tools found here, the site was home to the predecessors of modern man. Their descendants, the Bushmen, were the only tribe living here until the Iron Age Tonga people migrated from northern Zambia in the early 12th century. Living in thatched, pole, and mud huts, the Tonga were skilled in smelting, manufactured iron implements, and fired ceramic pots.

The high thatched roofs and rough walls of the Matetsi chalets recall the Tonga architecture. Roughly chiseled teak doors and burnished wrought-iron grates swing open along the full length of the suite, letting guests soak up breathtaking views of the mirrored surface of the Zambezi. Shaded by ancient mangosteen and waterberry trees, each suite has its own private plunge pool surrounded by local pottery. Combining modern minimalism with colonial chic, Conscorp's designers have, once again, raised bush luxury to new heights.

Any possibility of safari blues caused by the blue-washed walls
and iron doors is swept away by the mosquito netting draped languidly over the bed (below).
The classic combination of blue and white is given a new twist with custom-printed fabrics: Blue
leopard pillows are mixed with traditional African fabric imprinted with potato-stamped motifs.
Pool tiles and bed ties complement the color scheme (right).

river rush

"At Tongabezi and Sindabezi, we wanted a river retreat where guests could enjoy a slow pace after the adrenaline rush of Victoria Falls," owner Ben Parker explained. The adventure center of Africa, Victoria Falls draws busloads of travelers set on bungee jumping from the highest commercial jump in the world, Victoria Falls Bridge, and rafting on some of the world's wildest white-water rapids through the Batonga gorge 300 feet below.

Twelve miles upstream, the two camps retain the bucolic atmosphere that Livingstone experienced when he discovered the falls in 1855. Intent on converting the Zambezi River into "God's highway" to deliver European religion to central Africa, Livingstone canoed eastward toward the sea. Warned by the roar of the great waterfall that he had heard about, Livingstone landed on a small island, now called Livingstone Island, on the lip of the gorge.

"No one can imagine the beauty of the view," he wrote. "Scenes so lovely must have been gazed upon by angels in their flight." Now visitors line up for "Angel Flights" in noisy helicopters and bush planes.

Guided by Luther Peyton, a Tonga tribesman raised by a missionary family who is carrying on Livingstone's work, we drove from Tongabezi through the riverine rain forest to the crossing point to Livingstone Island. A motorized canoe whisked us downstream, past palm-dotted islands where elephants browsed and onto the riverbank where hippos wallowed. Following a dripping trail lined with African ebony and swarming with vervet monkeys and banded mongoose, we stepped out onto a verdant marsh permanently veiled in mist created as the Zambezi plunges into the gorge. As the sun sparkled through clouds of spray billowing so high they're visible 50 miles away, multiple rainbows arched over the chasm.

Indicating a spot where the river slowed, Luther said, "Let's walk across here." I adamantly refused, but relented as I watched a stream of visitors wade across. I splashed over to the rock pool where Luther was bathing. Pulling myself up onto the shelf formed by the gorge rocks, I looked down. Suddenly, I realized I was sitting on the edge (albeit quite securely) of Victoria Falls. I had marveled at Victoria Falls from a plane and ridden the roller-coaster ride through the gorge on raft, but, perched here on the cusp of the falls, I felt, as Livingstone had, like I was in the company of angels.

Like Conscorp's decorators, Ben Parker of Tongabezi took his cue for the design of his Zambezi riverside camp from the environment. But instead of focusing on the river water and rocks, he was inspired by the reeds and rushes that grow along the bank.

For centuries, these materials have been used by the local Tonga people to construct the roofs and cover the walls of their rondavels. The chalets and shower stalls at Tongabezi are a clever synthesis of reed boma and dagga rondavel built into the bank of the river.

*Chalets at Sindabezi
open onto a river porch.
Covered in reed matting,
the en suite wash basin
(left) harmonizes with
the rustic interior. At
night, netting cascades
from a ceiling support,
creating a bedroom island
within the boma (below
right and opposite page).*

ALONG THE ZAMBEZI IN ZAMBIA, PAUL THEROUX FOUND "THE OLD ETERNAL AFRICA, THE ONE LIVINGSTONE KNEW."
EVEN TODAY, THE EXPLORER WOULD FIND IT "INSTANTLY FAMILIAR, FOR SO LITTLE HAS CHANGED."

*An old-fashioned radio
telephone disguises a modern*

*intercom system that hooks
guest bomas with camp
headquarters.*

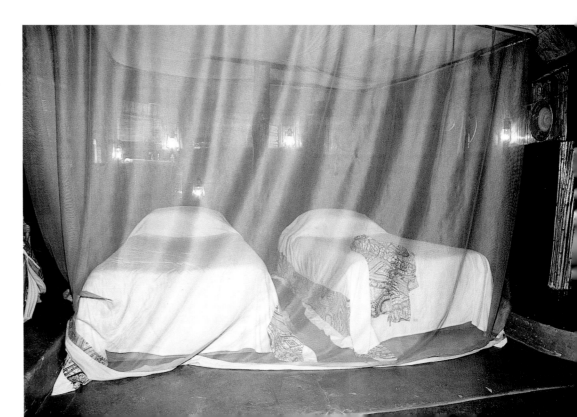

The tent bomas (left) and the
honeymoon suites (above)
were built by Ben Parker (below)
and his designer/partner, Will Ruck–
Keene, who died tragically in a car

accident. But his vision is carried on
by the staff at Tongabezi, its satellite
camp Sindabezi, and two tented
camps, Sausage Tree and
Potato Bush.

the queen of sheba's palace

On the pinnacle of another Zimbabwe landmark, German geologist Karl Mauch discovered in 1871 a massive 30-foot tower of smoothly cut granite blocks trimmed with cross-beams of intricately carved stone. He was convinced he had found the ruins of the biblical city Ophir, home of the Queen of Sheba. Instead he had found the remains of the greatest medieval city in sub-Saharan Africa, Great Zimbabwe.

Zimbabwe, meaning "great stone houses" in Shona, provides the architectural style for the nearby Lodge of the Ancient City. Like the ruins, it is approached through wonderfully curving, twisting walls of hand-hewn

Great Zimbabwe (upper left), which, in the 12th century, held sway over 20,000 people from eastern Zimbabwe into Botswana, Mozambique, and South Africa, inspired the architecture of the Lodge of the Ancient City.

granite block that either circumvent or incorporate mammoth boulders into the structure, resulting in an impressive harmony with the landscape.

Real and mythical creatures dart between outcroppings of rock and an overgrown garden. Turquoise and copper lizards sunbathing on chevron-patterned bricks inspired the color scheme for the interiors. Onyx and malachite Shona sculpture bursts from thickets and boulders. Zimbabwe's mascot, an avian described variously as a falcon, fish eagle, or mythological creature, presides here as it did more than 500 years ago, perched atop the Great Enclosure that housed a royal harem.

Like the surrounding rocks, the Lodge of the Ancient City's masonry abodes have a solid, settled feel. Like the shards of broken sculpture and remains of woven baskets half-hidden in the grass, the architecture ghosts the unsolved mystery of who built the Great Zimbabwe and what its history was.

Guest cottages mirror the
cattle herders' dagga huts
that encircled the Great
Enclosures: round mud
dwellings capped with
thatched cones.

Descendants of the stone-masons who created the Great Zimbabwe, Shona artists create mythical creatures and muses from black serpentine displayed in sculpture gardens such as Harare's Chapungu Kraal.

Like the builders of the Great Zimbabwe, the architects incorporated boulders and slopes into the design of the Main Lodge (right).

THE TRADITIONAL TRIANGULAR CHEVRON PATTERN OF THE GREAT ZIMBABWE ALSO DEC-ORATES THE WINDING PASSAGEWAYS LEADING TO THE GUEST COTTAGES AND THE MAIN LODGE'S CONICAL TOWER, A SMALL VERSION OF THE MYSTERIOUS PHALLIC STRUCTURES SCATTERED THROUGHOUT THE RUINS.

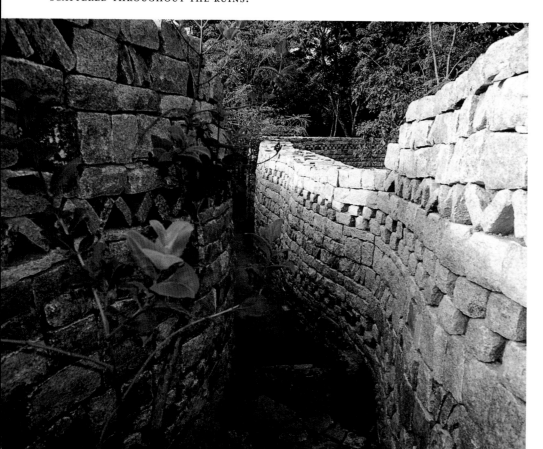

The bedrooms are modeled after the royal receiving room of Zimbabwe: The king, sprawled on an enormous bed on a raised platform, received subjects as they kneeled before a forged-iron railing.

THE DECOR ECHOES THE ANCIENT CIVILIZATION'S HANDIWORK IN IRON, GOLD, BRONZE, AND COPPER METALWORK, SOAPSTONE CARVINGS, AND CLAY POTTERY.

the stones of mt. kilimanjaro

It's no mystery why Richard and Tara Bonham built their stone haven in the isolated Chyulu Hills. "The beauty of this location is that we can roam over half a million acres and not see any signs of the 20th century," Richard explained. "It's like the Africa that our grandparents pioneered."

Richard's maternal grandfather, Arthur Trench, arrived at the turn of the century. After a hurricane leveled the family sugar plantation in Trench Town, Jamaica, Arthur resettled in Costa Rica, learning the emerging science of coffee farming. Joining his five brothers in Kenya, Arthur pioneered coffee cultivation in British East Africa and helped Karen Blixen when she embarked on her plantation endeavors.

Richard's paternal grandparents were English. His father, Jack Bonham, ran away to Kenya in 1920 and became a renowned game warden. At nine years old, Richard started accompanying his father on safari and is considered one of the top guides in Africa.

Tara is the granddaughter of one of Kenya's most famous professional hunters, J.A. Hunter, who at age 18 was banished from Scotland by his family, who were outraged by his relationship with an older woman. As his father bid farewell, he offered his son a gun, not his hand. It served him well: He became the best shot in Kenya, sought after by wealthy American clients, the

Kenyan Game Department, and even the Maasai, who "gave" him Ngorongoro Crater in appreciation for controlling the lions preying on their cattle.

Like Arthur Trench, J.A. Hunter was a contemporary of the legendary safari characters. The aviatrix Beryl Markham gave Tara riding lessons; Bror Blixen, Denys Finch Hatton, and Philip Percival were frequent guests. Hunter, in fact, was present at Finch Hatton's last meal, was the first to arrive at the site where Finch Hatton crashed, and accompanied his remains back to the Blixen home.

When Richard and Tara designed their lodge, they wanted to incorporate the drama of their grandfathers' days. An open wall in each guest cottage frames the view that epitomizes classic Africa.

Rising with the sun, I saw the barely visible outline of Mt. Kilimanjaro etched in the sky like a Zen painting. Floating above a translucent stroke of mist, its snow-capped peak reflected the pink rays of dawn, beckoning me like a landlocked lighthouse to climb the mountain Queen Victoria gave as a gift to her German cousin. I had struggled up the oxygen-poor atmosphere of Africa's highest mountain before, and I knew why its Chagga name means "impossible for the caravan to continue." Opting to ascend in Richard's bush plane, I looked down from 20,000 feet

At the foot of Mt. Kilimanjaro, Ol Donyu Wuas is one of Africa's most beautiful bush homes, represented for the Bonham family by Sandy and Chip Cunningham (opposite page) of Bush Homes/ African Safaris.

"As time approached for me to leave Oloasuai, I wondered how it would be to move away from this place where I felt alive as never before."

—Robert Vavra, *A Tent with a View*

on the view that I had not forgotten since my climb 20 years ago.

From as far as the eye could see stretched the plains of Africa. To the north were the settler homes of Kenya that I had visited in Lake Naivasha. To the east and west were the tented camps of the Masai Mara and the Serengeti. And to the south were the exciting new safari lands of Zimbabwe, Botswana, Zambia, and South Africa.

Contemplating all the characters I had met on safari, I recalled a comment of J.A. Hunter's. Asked what his contemporaries—the legendary settlers and professional hunters—were really like, he answered, "They were a race of giants."

Throughout my travels in Africa, I shared this impression of the successive generations that had inherited the safari legacy. From Kenya to South Africa, at every safari camp and game lodge, I met people differentiated by a commitment to the wilderness, a passion for adventure, and an appreciation of ethnic diversity.

On safari I had found there is more to discover than game: There is an ethic to share—to learn to welcome life, nature, and diversity with enthusiasm, good humor, and respect. As an old Arabic proverb states, "He who has not traveled (*safara*) does not fully appreciate life."

"*Were I not married with grandchildren, I should head back into Africa again, and end my days in the open air. It is useless to tell me of civilization. Take it from one who has tried both, there is charm in the wild life.*"

—WILLIAM COTTON OSWELL, SHORTLY BEFORE HIS DEATH

Walnut-stained wood floors provide
an elegant counterpoint to the high
thatched ceilings and natural vegetable-
dyed rugs. Massive polished trunks of
exotic wood have been crafted into
plump oversized beds. Local stones and
buffalo horns accessorize the bathroom.

Bringing Safari Home

*H*ome is the beginning of all journeys and the final destination. For many, homecoming is the best part of a trip. Returning from each trip, real or vicarious, we can weave the magic of the voyage into our home. Certainly, putting up trophies has always been a high point of safari, although prints and carvings have replaced skins and skulls.

But you don't need to travel across the ocean to bring safari home. "Just take a trip to local shops and let your imagination go wild!" said John Tripp, Los Angeles decorator, caterer, and co-owner of St. Andrews Place, who learned to create dramatic environments by working with professionals such as the renowned New York caterer/designer Donald Bruce White.

"You mean I've just traveled all over Africa to capture a look anyone can duplicate?" I said.

"I'll bet your last chapter that I can," John replied. And that's how John took on safari.

I set the guidelines—and then all I set were f-stops. Rule One: We had to rely on easily available, affordable products. Rule Two: We had to focus on an average house—mine. Rule Three: True to the style of the quintessential fly-camps, we had to create environments that could be erected and dismantled on a whim, relying on nothing more elaborate than open space and four walls.

"Whatever you take your lead from, let your imagination be your guide," John said. "When guests visit your home, the decor should unveil your personality gradually, taking the visitor on a journey as they discover your unique character.

"Ultimately, it's the values of hospitality, originality, and self-knowledge that, more than accessories and furniture, convey the savoir faire that is the essence of safari chic."

Using tiki torches from Home Depot, lanterns from Cost Plus, and mosquito netting from Pier One, John Tripp transformed the author's backyard hillside into a California sundowner setting. Old rugs, trunks, and Swahili fabrics add to the *Out of Africa* ambience.

"Home is not the same when we come
back from a trip or close a book."
—Annie Gottlieb, *Voyage to Paradise*

The author's son and friends
were game for safari, too.
John Tripp carried out the
kitchen table and covered
it with a sheet of fresh sod.
We left the grass on the hill

long and wild, but tamed
the tabletop with bright
zebra-patterned place
mats from South Africa,
distributed on the Internet
(www.safarichic.com).
Carved wooden zebras,
animal napkin rings, and
bumblebee pencils from
Cost Plus, along with
additional party favors
from Pier One, provided
an inexpensive party buzz.

In a North Hollywood patio, John Tripp created a stunning safari sala. The canvas canopy, kilim pillows, and antique silver evoked the look of Cottar's 1920 Camp. The tasteful combination of Balinese folding chairs, Malabar lantern, and tribal art is reminiscent of Abu Camp and Londolozi Tree Camp. Especially effective in this small backyard is the use of a mirror and tiki torches placed behind matchstick blinds to create an illusion of greater space.

Treasures from safari combine with local merchandise to evoke the magic of Africa. Elegant place mats from South Africa, framed prints from photographer Horst Klemm, and African tribal art, distributed on the Internet site www.safarichic.com, fire up memories of safari nights.

"WE BRING BACK FROM OUR TRAVELS THINGS THAT WILL BRING OUR TRAVELS BACK TO US," WROTE ANNIE GOTTLIEB. "*SOUVENIR* MEANS, LITERALLY, A MEMORY." JOHN TRIPP RE-CREATED THE ESSENCE OF THE AFRICAN SAVANNA WITH A TABLE SETTING OF ANTIQUE BRASS CUTLERY FROM POTTERY BARN, AMETHYST GLASSES FROM COST PLUS, WOODEN GIRAFFES FROM PIER ONE, AND A CENTER-PIECE OF DWARF PAPYRUS ADRIFT IN A STREAM OF RIVER ROCKS ILLUMINATED WITH CONCEALED VOTIVE CANDLES.

Animal print linens from Garnet Hill complement a Galdessa-inspired table made from Arizona flagstone (right). A Botswana basket has been fashioned into a classic flower arrangement (above). Tea lights illuminate a crocodile skull from Evolution to capture the gripping adventure of the bush (below, left); nestled inside Pottery Barn's traveling candle holder, they reflect the classic romance of safari (below, right).

Recalling the proclivity of collapsible, multipurpose furniture used on safari, John Tripp fashioned two very different safari chic bedrooms using easily available products

such as storage shelving from Hold Everything and bed linen from Restoration Hardware (left) to mosquito netting from Ikea and a chandelier from a swap meet (right).

SAFARI GUIDE

For more information on these camps, or to preview and order an expanded video and CD-ROM of Africa's best safari camps, visit **http://www.safarichic.com** *on the Internet.*

SAFARI OPERATORS

ABERCROMBIE AND KENT
1520 Kensington Rd.
Oak Brook, IL 60521
Phone: 800–323–7308
Fax: 708–954–2944
e-mail: info@abercrombiekent.com

BUSH HOMES/AFRICAN SAFARIS
887 West Marietta St. NW
Studio S-101
Atlanta, GA 30318
Phone: 404–888–0909
Fax: 404–588–9961
e-mail: bushhomes@aol.com
P.O. Box 56923
Nairobi, Kenya
Phone: 254–2–571647/571649
Fax: 254–2–571665

SAFARI SOLO
21800 Dumetz Rd.
Woodland Hills, CA 91365
Phone: 818–999–0202
Fax: 818–999–0202
e-mail: solo@safarichic.com

CLASSIC SAFARI CAMPS OF AFRICA
P.O. Box 244
Northriding 2162, South Africa
Phone: 27–11–465–6427
Fax: 27–11–465–9309
e-mail: classics@pop.onwe.co.za

CONSERVATION CORPORATION OF AFRICA
P.O. Box 650039
Miami, FL 33265-0039
Phone: 888–882–3742
Fax: 305–221–3223
e-mail: scarrillo@conscorpusa.com

MELLIFERA BOOKINGS
P.O. Box 24397
Nairobi, Kenya
Phone: 254–2–574689
Fax: 254–2–564945

KENYA

COTTARS' BUSH HOME
P.O. Box 44191
Nairobi, Kenya
Phone: 254–2–884508/882408
Fax: 254–2–882234
e-mail: cottars@form-net.com

COTTAR'S 1920S CAMP
See Cottars' Bush Home

FINCH HATTON'S CAMP
Peter Frank
P. O. Box 24423
Nairobi, Kenya
Phone: 254–2–604321-2
Fax: 254–2–604323

GALDESSA
Pierre Mourgue d'Algue
P.O. Box 24397, Nairobi, Kenya
Phone: 254–2–574689 or 567251
Fax: 254–2–564945
e-mail: pierre@galdessa.com

GIRAFFE MANOR
Rick and Bryony Anderson
P.O. Box 15004
Langata, Nairobi, Kenya
Phone: 254–2–891078
Fax: 254–2–890949
e-mail: giraffe@form-net.com

GOVERNOR'S CAMPS
P.O. Box 48217
Nairobi, Kenya
Phone: 254–2–331871
Fax: 254–2–726427
e-mail: govscamp@africaonline.co.ke

KONGONI GAME RESERVE
P.O. Box 15026
Nairobi, Kenya
Phone: 254–2–890184/890444
Fax: 254–2–890096

LONGONOT RANCH HOUSE
Safaris Unlimited (Africa) Ltd.
P.O. Box 24181, Nairobi, Kenya
Phone: 254–2–891168/890435
Fax: 254–2–891113
e-mail: safunlim@africaonline.co.ke

NGONG HOUSE
P.O. Box 24963
Nairobi, Kenya
Phone: 254–2–890840
Fax: 254–2–890674
e-mail: ngonghouse@form-net.com

NORFOLK HOTEL
P.O. Box 58581
Nairobi, Kenya
Phone: 254–2–216940
Fax: 254–2–216796

OL DONYU WUAS
P.O. Box 24133
Nairobi, Kenya
Phone: 254–2–882521/884475
Fax: 254–2–882728
e-mail: bonham.luke@swiftkenya.com

SEKANANI TENTED CAMP
P.O. Box 15010
Nairobi, Kenya
Phone: 254–2–212370–12
Fax: 254–2–228875

**SIROCCO HOUSE &
OLERAI COTTAGE**
P.O. Box 54667
Nairobi, Kenya
Phone: 254–2–334868/242572
Fax: 254–2–332106/890441
e-mail: oria@iconnect.co.ke

ZAMBIA

TONGABEZI AND SINDABEZI
Private Bag 31
Livingstone, Zambia
Phone: 260–3–323235/323296
Fax: 260–3–323224/324208
e-mail: tonga@zamnet.zm

ZIMBABWE

GOLIATH SAFARI AND CANOEING TRIPS
Bronte Hotel
P.O. Box Ch 294 Chisipiti
Harare, Zimbabwe
Phone: 263-4-739836/7/8
Fax: 263-4-708843
e-mail: goliath@harare.iafrica.com

TOUCH OF THE WILD
Private Bag 6, Hillside
Bulawayo, Zimbabwe
Phone: 263–9–44566/7 or 72
Fax: 263–9–29088
e-mail: touchwld@harare.iafrica.com

TANZANIA

KUSINI CAMP OF THE SERENGETI AND SWALA CAMP OF THE TARANGIRE
Machado Luxury Tented Camps
P.O. Box 14823
Arusha, Tanzania
Phone: 255–57–6585/4231
Fax: 255–57–8020
e-mail: kiboko@habari.com.Tz

BOTSWANA

ABU CAMP
Private Bag 332
Maun, Botswana
Phone: 267–661260
Fax: 267–661005
e-mail: ebs@info.bw

AUDI CAMP
P.O. Box 28
Maun, Botswana
Phone: 267-660-599
Fax: 267-660-581
e-mail: audicamp@info.bw

JACK'S CAMP
P.O. Box 173
Francistown, Botswana
Phone: 267-212277
Fax: 267-213458
e-mail: unchart@info.bw

ODDBALL'S
P.O. Box 21
Maun, Botswana
Phone: 267-660-220
Fax: 267-660-589
e-mail: oddballs@info.bw

SOUTH AFRICA

GREENLIFE OF SOUTH AFRICA
P.O. Box 48114
Kammetjie, Cape Town, 7976
South Africa
Phone: 27–21–780–1391
Fax: 27–21–780–1309

MALAMALA AND KIRKMAN'S HOMESTEAD
P.O. Box 2575, Randburg, 2125
South Africa
Phone: 27–11–789–2677
Fax: 27–11–886–4382
e-mail: jhb@malamala.co
Website: www.malamala.com

SAVANNA TENTED CAMP
P.O. Box 3619
White River, South Africa, 1240
Phone: 27–13–751–2205
Fax: 27–13–751–2204
e-mail: ecologics@soft.co.za

LONDOLOZI TREE CAMP AND LONDOLOZI MAIN CAMP
CCA, Bateleur House
Private Bag 27, Benmore 2210
South Africa
Phone: 27–11–784–7077
Fax: 27–11–784–7667
e-mail:reservations@conscorp.co.za

SAFARI MARKETPLACE

Shop for safari-style designer accessories, photographic prints and calendars, and ethnic art on the Internet at

http://www.safarichic.com

TENTS AND SAFARI FURNITURE

BRITISH KHAKI
62 Greene St.
New York, NY 10012
Phone: 212–343–2299

MALABAR COAST
8650 Hayden Pl.
Culver City, CA 90232
Phone: 310–558–5000
Website: www.malacoast.com

R & R DESIGN IMPORTS
3830 S. Broadway
Los Angeles, CA 90037
Phone: 213–231–4347

HOME FURNISHINGS

ANTHROPOLOGIE
210 W. Lancaster Ave.
Wayne, PA 19087
Phone: 610–687–4141

COST PLUS
201 Clay St.
Oakland, CA 94607
Phone: 510–893–7300

CRATE & BARREL
725 Landwehr Rd.
Northbrook, IL 60062
For catalog, call 1–800–451–8217

IKEA
496 W. Germantown Pike
Plymouth Meeting, PA 19462
For catalog, call 1–800–434–4532

HOLD EVERYTHING
3250 Van Ness Ave.
San Francisco, CA 94109
For catalog, call 1–800–421–2285

LYNN CHASE DESIGNS
381 Park Ave. South
New York, NY 10016
For catalog, call 1–800–228–9909

PIER ONE IMPORTS
For catalog, call 1–800–447–4371
Website: www.pier1.com

POTTERY BARN
P.O. Box 7044
San Francisco, CA 94120
For catalog, call 1–800–922–5507

HOME FURNISHINGS
(CONT'D)

RESTORATION HARDWARE
15 Koch Rd., Suite J
Corte Madera, CA 94925
For catalog, call 1–800–762–1005

DECO JAZZ
20 Roadnight Rd.
Greyville, Durban, 4001
South Africa
e-mail: saunders@aol.com

GARNET HILL (MAIL ORDER)
231 Main St.
Franconia, NH 03580
For catalog, call 1–800–622–6216

THE SILK TRADING CO.
360 S. La Brea Ave.
Los Angeles, CA 90036
Phone: 323–954–9280

TUFENKIAN IMPORT-EXPORT
902 Broadway
New York, NY 10010
Phone: 212–475–2475

EVOLUTION
120 Spring St.
New York, NY 10012
Phone: 212–343–1114
Website: www.evolution.com

ETHNIC ART

AFRICAN ARTS, ETC.
2019 Pontius Ave.
Los Angeles, CA 90025
Phone: 310-312-0069

AFRICAN ODYSSEY
125 E. Palace Ave.
Santa Fe, NM 87501
Phone: 505–820–7377
e-mail: AfricanOdyssey.com/santafe

BUSHCRAFT TRADING
43 Juta St., Braamfontein,
Johannesburg, South Africa
Phone: 011–27–11–403–2744
Fax: 011–27–11–403–1914

CENTER FOR AFRICAN
AMERICAN ARTS
2221 Peachtree Rd., Suite D341
Atlanta, GA 30309
Phone: 404–605–0734

ERIC ROBERTSON
AFRICAN ARTS
36 W. 22nd St.
New York, NY 10010
Phone: 212–675–4045

STUDIO AFRICANA
P.O. Box 48
Victoria Falls, Zimbabwe
Phone: 011–263–9–4244

WINDOWS TO AFRICA
5210 S. Harper Ct.
Chicago, IL 60615
Phone: 312–955–7742

SAFARI OUTFITTERS
AND CLOTHES

EX-OFFICIO
1419 Elliot Ave. West
Seattle, WA 98119
For catalog, call 1–800–833–0831

HOLLAND & HOLLAND
50 E. 57th St.
New York, NY 10012
Phone: 212–752–7755

—

442 N. Rodeo Dr.
Beverly Hills, CA 90210
Phone: 310–271–1100

WILLIS & GEIGER OUTFITTERS
1902 Explorers Trail
Reedsburg, WI 53959
For catalog, call 1–800–223–1408

WILDLIFE FOUNDATIONS

AFRICAN WILDLIFE FOUNDATION
1400 16th St. NW, #120
Washington, DC 20036
Phone: 888–945–3543
Fax: 202–939–3332
e-mail: awf.org@igc.apc.org
Website: www.awf.org
Tax Exempt ID Number:
52–0781390

AFRICAN FUND FOR ENDANGERED WILDLIFE, INC.
4602 Waterfall Ct., #L
Owings Mills, MD 21117
Phone: 410–581–8116
Fax: 410–581–4993
e-mail: giraffem@erols.com

THE GALLMANN MEMORIAL FOUNDATION
P.O. Box 45593, Nairobi, Kenya
Fax: 254–2–521220

RURAL INVESTMENT FUND
CCA, Bateleur House
Private Bag 27, Benmore 2210
South Africa
Phone: 27–11–784–7077
Fax: 27–11–784–7667
e-mail: anthea@conscorp.co.za

SAVE THE ELEPHANTS
P.O. Box 6388
Snowmass Village, CO 81615
Phone: 970–923–2466
Fax: 970–923–2467
Tax Exempt ID Number:
74–2488671

CREDITS AND ENDNOTES

Map (12-13) © 1995 HarperCollins Publishers Ltd. Reproduced by permission.

Thank you to these photographers for providing the following images:

Gordon Church: 3, 54 (lower right), 55

Horst Klemm: Front cover, 79 (upper and lower right), 109 (top and bottom), 110 (bottom), 111 (bottom), 112-115 (all), 120 (top)

Herman Pogieter: 151 (lower right)

The Golden Age of Safari

1. Much of the information in this chapter was provided from Bartle Bull's *Safari: A Chronicle of Adventure* (Penguin Group, London, 1988), an expertly researched, well-written, and entertaining history of African safari trends and personalities.

The Quintessential Fly-Camp

1. This and many other fascinating facts are contained in Errol Trzebinski's *The Kenya Pioneers* (William Heinemann Ltd., London, 1985), an overview of the settler movement that reads more like a novel than the in-depth historical analysis that it is.

2. For expert coverage of the intriguing science of tracking and Bushman lore, refer to Louis Liebenberg's *The Art of Tracking: The Origin of Science* (David Philip Publishers, South Africa, 1990).

Hunter Homesteads

1. See The Quintessential Fly-Camp: 1, above

2. Errol Trzebinski's *Silence Will Speak* (University of Chicago Press, Chicago, 1997) is the gripping nonfiction account of Karen Blixen's relationship with Denys Finch Hatton, which formed the basis for her book and the movie *Out of Africa*.

For more information about these and other recommended books, please refer to the bibliography.

BIBLIOGRAPHY

Algotsson, Sharne, Denys Davis, and Yanick Rice Lamb. *The Spirit of African Design.* New York: Clarkson Potter, 1996.

Beard, Peter. *The End of the Game: The Last Word From Paradise.* San Francisco: Chronicle Books, 1988.

———. *Longing for Darkness: Kamante's Tales from Out of Africa.* San Francisco: Chronicle Books, 1990.

Bull, Bartle. *Safari: A Chronicle of Adventure.* London: Penguin Group, 1988.

Douglas-Hamilton, Iain and Oria. *Among the Elephants.* London: Collins & Harvill Press, 1975.

Estes, Richard D. *The Behavior Guide to African Mammals.* Berkeley: University of California Press, 1991.

———. *The Safari Companion.* Post Mills, Vermont: Chelsea Green Publishing Company, 1993.

Fisher, Angela. *Africa Adorned.* New York: Harry N. Abrams, 1984.

Gallmann, Kuki. *I Dreamed of Africa.* London: Penguin Books, 1991.

Gottlieb, Annie, and Thomas McKnight. *Voyage to Paradise: A Visual Odyssey.* New York: HarperCollins, 1993.

Hallet, Jean Pierre, with Alex Pelle. *Animal Kitabu.* New York: Random House, 1967.

Hemingway, Ernest. *The Green Hills of Africa.* New York: Scribner Classics, 1998.

Heminway, John. *African Journeys: A Personal Guidebook.* New York: Warner Books, 1990.

———. *The Imminent Rains.* Boston: Little, Brown, 1969.

———. *No Man's Land: A Personal Journey Into Africa.* New York: E.P. Dutton, 1982, 1983.

Hepburn, Katharine. *The Making of The African Queen.* New York: Alfred A. Knopf, 1987.

Hunter, J.A., and Daniel Mannix. *Tales of the African Frontier.* New York: Harper & Brothers, 1954.

Huxley, Elspeth. *The Flame Trees of Thika: Memories of an African Childhood.* New York: William Morrow and Company, 1959.

Joubert, Beverly and Dereck. *Hunting with the Moon.* Washington, D.C.: National Geographic Society, 1997.

Klemm, Horst. *An African Journal.* Auckland Park, R.S.A.: Horst Klemm, 1994.

Lanting, Frans, with Christine Eckstrom and Alexandra Arrowsmith (editors). *Okavango: Africa's Last Eden.* San Francisco: Chronicle Books, 1993.

Leakey, Louis Seymour Bazett. *White African: An Early Autobiography.* Cambridge, Massachusetts: Scenkman Publishing, 1966.

Liebenberg, Louis. *The Art of Tracking: The Origin of Science.* South Africa: David Philip Publishers, 1990.

Markham, Beryl. *West With the Night.* Boston: Houghton Mifflin, 1942.

Matthiessen, Peter. *The Tree Where Man Was Born.* New York: E.P. Dutton, 1972

Moss, Cynthia. *Portraits in the Wild: Animal Behavior in East Africa.* Chicago: University of Chicago Press, 1982.

Owens, Delia and Mark. *Cry of the Kalahari.* London: Collins, 1985.

Rattray, Gillian. *To Everything There Is a Season: The Story of a Game Reserve.* Johannesburg: Jonathon Ball, 1986.

Ricciardi, Mirella. *Vanishing Africa.* London: Collins, 1971.

Turle, Gillies, with Mark Greenberg and Peter Beard. *The Art of the Maasai.* New York: Alfred A. Knopf, 1992.

Trzebinski, Errol. *The Kenya Pioneers.* London: William Heinemann Ltd., 1985.

———. *Silence Will Speak: A Study of the Life of Denys Finch Hatton and his Relationship with Karen Blixen.* Chicago: University of Chicago Press, 1997.

Van der Post, Laurens, and Jane Taylor. *Testament to the Bushmen.* Middlesex, England: Penguin Books, 1984.

Vavra, Robert. *A Tent With a View: An Intimate African Experience.* New York: William Morrow, 1991.

BIBI JORDAN *on safari.*

In photographs and editorial, *Safari Chic* conveys the intoxicating appeal of the wild settings, original styles and eclectic personalities that first lured me to Africa. For lovers of design, travel and sheer *'joie de vivre,' Safari Chic* is a must!
—Peter Beard
The End of the Game, Eyelids of Dawn, and *Fifty Years of Portrait*

Safari Chic is a beautifully illustrated book which shows how caringly-created interiors that blend with their environment enrich life experiences. Whether you are embarking on decorating your dream house or departing for a dream safari, *Safari Chic* ensures you'll reach your destination in style.
—Richard Estes
Safari Companion

Before I saw this book, I wouldn't have been confident that 'safari' and 'chic' were to be uttered in the same breath. I now know that had I stuck to my guns, I would have been blind to a new adventure.
—John Heminway
Africa Journeys: A Personal Guidebook and *The Imminent Rains*

A unique book-experience ... [W]ith spectacular photographs, provocative stories and exciting personalities, we are taken on a journey of adventure and romance sufficient to instill our own desire to design at home our own safari chic.
—Alexandra Stoddard
Creating a Beautiful Home and *Gracious Living in a New World*